THE OFFICIAL
Rugby League Yearbook
1988–89

THE OFFICIAL

Rugby League Yearbook
1988–89

SPONSORED BY BRITISH COAL

Heinemann Kingswood

Heinemann Kingswood
Michelin House, 81 Fulham Road, London SW3 6RB

LONDON   MELBOURNE   AUCKLAND

Copyright © 1988 Heinemann Kingswood except for the 1988–89 fixtures which
remain the copyright © 1988 the Rugby Football League

First published 1988
ISBN 0 434 981648

Photoset, printed and bound in Great Britain
by Redwood Burn Limited, Trowbridge, Wiltshire

Contents

Acknowledgements 6

Preface *by David Oxley* 7
Chief Executive, the Rugby Football League

Foreword *by Sir Robert Haslam* 9
Chairman, the British Coal Corporation

1 The 1987–88 Season

    1 The Internationals 13
      Paul Fitzpatrick

    2 The Stones Bitter Championship 28
      and Premiership Trophies
      Trevor Watson

    3 The Silk Cut Challenge Cup 45
      and the John Player Special Trophy
      Paul Wilson

    4 The British Coal Nines Tournament 64
      Ray French

    5 The Grünhalle Lager Lancashire Cup 70
      and the John Smith's Yorkshire Cup
      Mike Rylance

    6 Five Players of the Season 79
      Trevor Watson

    7 The Amateur Game 84
      Ron Girvin

    Appendixes: 1987–88 89

2 The Great Britain Whitbread Trophy Tour 95
    of Papua New Guinea, Australia
    and New Zealand, May-July 1988
    Ray French

3 Looking Ahead 1988–89
    A Preview of the Season 131
    Harry Edgar

    The 1988–89 Fixtures 143

    The Rugby Football League Clubs Directory 149

Acknowledgements

All the photographs, except two,
in this book have been reproduced
by kind permission of the Andrew Varley
Picture Agency.
The exceptions are those of Brendan Hill on p.80
by permission of Yorkshire Newspapers
and of Wigan St Patrick's on p.87
by permission of John Leatherbarrow.

The publishers are indebted also to Mike Rylance,
whose generous help at several stages of the book's
production was invaluable.

Preface

David Oxley
Chief Executive, the Rugby Football League

The Rugby League season of 1987–88, captured in the pages which follow, was a season packed with incident, drama, thrills and outstanding entertainment. The international nature of the game was emphasised by the early season tour of the Papua New Guinea Kumuls, the short visit by the Auckland representative side, and the historic unofficial world club championship match between Wigan and Manly. Certainly no one who was present at Central Park on that seething October evening will ever forget the epic game they were privileged to watch.

A John Player Trophy competition of sustained quality was quickly followed by high drama in the successive rounds of the Challenge Cup, the final of which produced yet another commanding performance from the outstanding Wigan team. Premiership-finals day at Old Trafford in May was another huge success with the second division battle between Oldham and Featherstone producing an outstanding game of great skill and sustained excitement. Widnes were worthy winners of the Stones Bitter Premiership and the League Championship, the culmination of a highly competitive and entertaining programme which saw massive increases of 20% and 40% respectively in attendances at first and second division league matches.

There were high hopes for the 1988 Lions tour 'down under' but a cruel and unprecedented spate of injuries before departure and during the tour inevitably took a dreadful toll. Nevertheless, everyone involved in the game looks forward to the approaching season with eager anticipation, especially after that great win in the third test in Sydney.

I am delighted that Rugby League's newest major sponsors, British Coal, have agreed to support this splendid *Official Yearbook*. British Coal's initiative in sponsoring the exciting and popular inaugural nine-a-side tournament and their generous investment in the vital area of youth rugby is greatly appreciated by all lovers of Rugby League. Our newest sponsors have rapidly become our close friends and we look forward with them to many more years working together in a happy and mutually beneficial relationship.

Foreword

Sir Robert Haslam
Chairman, the British Coal Corporation

Of all contemporary spectator sports, Rugby League is the one with most appeal for miners and mining folk. Its gritty, uncompromising image has much in common with the miner's character. It is invariably played hard with speed and skills that are a revelation, and a sporting discipline that is the envy of the followers and administrators of our other national sports.

In the Rugby League heartland are the coalfields of my native Lancashire, Yorkshire and Cumbria. Throughout the League's history, miners have always been well represented among the game's heroes. Their families are among its most devoted supporters. One of the great occasions in the nation's sporting calendar is the Rugby League Challenge Cup final, with mining people prominent in the many thousands who invade London for their big day-out. The sportsmanship and good humour of the crowd are infectious, and the match is renowned as one of the few capacity-crowd tournaments at which the capital's forces of law and order can carry out their duties with a smile.

Apart from our sponsorship of this excellent *Yearbook*, the most important contribution we are making is to the future of the game through our support of the exciting pro-am development programme at school and youth levels. British Coal is sponsoring the Rugby League Foundation to the extent of £120,000 over three years. A major part of this sponsorship will be the introduction of the British Coal National Youth League, an elite Under-19 midweek league involving district representative sides based on advanced training centres. Our backing will be in the form of finance for establishing centres of excellence and advanced training for young players, as well as travel grants and help in funding a general development programme for the game.

Another British Coal initiative is our sponsorship of a pioneering nine-a-side tournament with £25,000 in prizes. Held for the first time at Central Park, Wigan, in October 1987, the British Coal Nines proved a spectacular success. Eight top teams thrilled an appreciative crowd on the terraces and the many thousands more who watched the televised event in BBC's *Sportsnight* programme.

I shared the delight of the Rugby Football League's chairman, Bob Ashby, in the enthusiastic reception given to this inaugural venture and look forward to the Nines becoming an established event in Rugby League's calendar.

These recent initiatives not only reflect the 'New Face of British Coal' – my industry's current promotional slogan – but are a sign of Rugby League's enterprise and the game's continuing progress and development. I look forward to a long and rewarding association between the Rugby League and British Coal. May our two organisations prosper together in the years ahead.

9

I

The 1987–88 Season

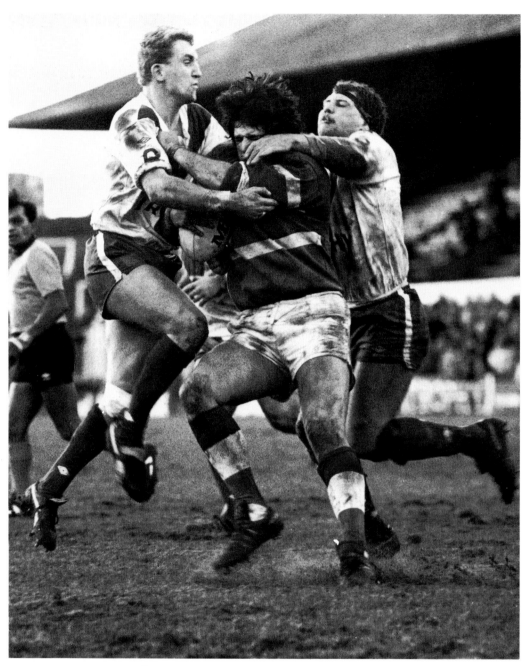

Shaun Edwards and Kevin Beardmore in
action in the Headingley Test against France.
Edwards was selected for the Lions' tour of
Australasia but he damaged a knee so seriously
in the first seven minutes of the Papua New
Guinea Test, that he returned to Britain
without taking any further part in the tour.

ONE

The Internationals

Paul Fitzpatrick

The problem was not unfamiliar: a tour of Australia (as well as Tests in Papua New Guinea and New Zealand) looming and too few international opportunities available for Malcolm Reilly, the Great Britain coach, to assess his country's playing strength. Previous national coaches would appreciate the frustrations.

Reilly had to make do with a home Test against Papua New Guinea in October 1987; a representative match against Auckland the same month; and two Tests against France in the spring of 1988, as well as two Under-21 games against the same opposition. When you are trying to fill twenty-six vacancies that is not a lot of international football. But at least Reilly was in a more fortunate position than Frank Myler, who had been coach on the previous tour to Australia. Myler had been left with the task of trying to repair the damage inflicted upon the British game by the 1982 Kangaroos, of imperishable memory. Some of his choices for the 1984 tour look, at this distance, surprising to say the least. But then Myler did not have an abundance of outstanding players at his disposal. Neither did Reilly but he had a few more than Myler.

Britain's rehabilitation as a world force in Rugby League had taken place under Maurice Bamford who had overseen three encouraging performances against New Zealand in 1985. Much of the optimism generated by that series evaporated a year later when Wally Lewis's 1986 Kangaroos completed their whitewash of the British at Old Trafford, Elland Road, and Wigan.

The third Test, however, suggested that Britain were drawing closer to Australia in skill, fitness, and commitment than at any time since 1978 – the last occasion on which Britain had beaten them. When Bamford announced his retirement soon after that game he bequeathed to his successor a useful squad, better organised and tougher mentally and physically than some of its predecessors.

It was no great surprise, then, that in the 1987–88 season Great Britain should win their three Whitbread Tests convincingly. Papua New Guinea betrayed their lack of experience in losing 0–42 at Wigan and although France showed a new spirit they were beaten 14–28 at Avignon and 12–30 at Headingley. But those games tended to show that victory, while always welcome, is not everything and Reilly was left with plenty to ponder before announcing his tour party.

Many reputations were already well established. A few more were enhanced, but not perhaps as many as Reilly would have liked. Paul Medley, the young Leeds second-row forward, won the man-of-the-match award on his first Test appearance against Papua. Against France in Avignon Hugh Waddell, the only second division player in the side, took the man-of-the-match award on his debut, making few mistakes in a game riddled with them. He was less effective in the return at Headingley but had shown the ability to traverse the divide between club football with Oldham and the international side. Steve Hampson, the Wigan full-back, was another to improve his standing.

One of the most controversial of Reilly's decisions was to select Martin Offiah, the Widnes left wing, playing in his first season of professional football, for the Avignon Test, and then leave him out at Leeds. Offiah, a former Rugby Union player with Rosslyn Park, was still patently raw. But his incisive finishing was one of the outstanding features of the season. He scored, on debut, a try in France but was replaced by David Plange for the return game and for the first time possibly since he took over the national side Reilly had left himself open to accusations of bias. The 22-year-old Plange was from Reilly's former club at Castleford. He was a tough competitor and an effective finisher but it was hard to see what purpose was served in omitting Offiah. He was obviously in need of more big-game practice. But he would not acquire that if he did not play.

The most heartening aspect of the season was to see the French team recover some health. During the 1986–87 season the 13-a-side game had looked on the verge of extinction there and the international at Carcassonne, Malcolm Reilly's second game in charge of the Great Britain side, was chaotic even by French standards. Only four hours before the game, France's coach, Tas Baitieri, an Italian-born Australian, was sacked, much to the anger of the French players. They threatened to boycott the match but were persuaded not to do so by the youthful Baitieri, showing commendable maturity in a heated situation. In the background there was more turbulence with Jacques Soppelsa, president of the French Rugby League, being ousted from office. Revelations of the game's parlous financial state did nothing to dispel the sense of crisis.

The game itself was a disgrace, an unsavoury affair in which Mike Gregory, the Warrington forward, had his nose broken by a punch from Jean-Luc Rabot – an offence which, ludicrously, cost the Frenchman ten minutes in the sin-bin – and Pierre Aillères was sent off for boring knees first into Garry Schofield while the British player lay on the ground. From this nadir the sport seemed able to go only one of two ways – out of existence or upwards. Thankfully, it began the climb back to respectability. Soppelsa was replaced; Baitieri was given a role within the game in liaison and public relations as well as acting as player-manager, with huge enthusiasm, for the second division club Paris–Châtillon; an injection of government money helped stave off the immediate financial problems; and Jacques Jorda, coach at St Estève, was placed in charge of the national side.

In a country dominated by Rugby Union, international results are vitally important to a Rugby League side struggling for newspaper coverage, sponsors and television exposure. France gained some encouragement by beating Papua New Guinea in October 1987, and although that win was then followed by two defeats against Britain their displays in those games were little short of a revelation considering the problems of the previous year. The Avignon Test, especially, produced the most enjoyable and entertaining of games. Discipline on both sides was excellent and, although Britain's 28 points constituted a record on French soil, the margin of victory was harsh indeed on the French. And while France were well beaten in the return game at Headingley there was encouraging evidence that the revival was not about to collapse.

Avignon, 24 January

France 14 Great Britain 28

Great Britain went into this Whitbread Test with three newcomers in their side: Paul Loughlin, Martin Offiah, and Hugh Waddell, who was to emerge with the man-of-the-match award after an afternoon of good, honest endeavour. There were many mistakes, from both sides, and enough from Britain's point of view to be alarming. Similar blunders committed at Lang Park, Brisbane, or at Sydney, would be to invite punishment. But putting such thoughts aside, and judging it in isolation, the match was a splendid advertisement for international football, one of the most entertaining between the countries in my experience.

France's coach, Jacques Jorda, whose St Estève side had reached the French Cup final playing open, enterprising football, had promised a new approach. It proved to be no idle claim. The discipline of the French was admirable and they concentrated on what they do best: running and skilful handling. With a New Zealand referee, Neville Kesha, keen to maintain the game's flow a crowd of 6,000 was rewarded with eighty minutes of entertaining, if flawed, football.

Much of France's inspiration stemmed from half-back, where Dominique Espugna and Gilles Dumas formed an efficient partnership. Vigorous running, imaginative tactics and skilled handling opened up the British defence on a number of occasions. With the pack, to a man, performing creditably the French were in with a chance of victory until the final minutes when two unexpected tries put the British out of sight.

All five of Britain's tries were scored by their backs, two of them from unusually long range. But mistakes were made in both defence and attack with the Great Britain captain, Ellery Hanley, one of the chief culprits. Twice in the first half he should have created tries. The first time he clung on to the ball when a pass to Drummond, unmarked on his outside, would have practically guaranteed a touchdown. Soon afterwards, Hanley seemed certain to score himself but then threw out a wild pass which went to ground. In the second half he looked to be in the clear but, surprisingly for a man with such a relish for try-scoring, appeared to run out of self-belief and was tackled short of the line. As Malcolm Reilly said later: at this level you simply cannot afford to scorn chances such as those. And there were others.

A promising, opening flourish by the French ended disappointingly for home followers with their side 6 points in arrears. From inside his own '25' Schofield drew in the French cover and then released Drummond on a run of eighty yards which took the winger round the edge of the French defence. He then cut across towards the posts to give Loughlin an easy goal. A second try from Schofield, after a crossfield passing move involving Edwards, Hanley and Hampson, took Britain into a lead of 10–4 at the interval, Dumas having kicked two penalties for France. But one of many British mistakes at the start of the second half brought France 4 points and a large measure of encouragement.

15

From the kick-off, Drummond knocked on. France won the scrum and from close range Tisseyre turned inside to send in Verdes, stampeding up on the left. Dumas was given a simple kick at goal but in his excitement, possibly, squandered an inviting opportunity to equalise. There followed one of the most exciting passages of the contest. A penalty from Loughlin put Britain 12–8 ahead and then a clever piece of midfield work by Edwards helped to take the score to 18–8. Edwards chipped the ball over the defence, followed up and retrieved it, and then threw a swift pass – marginally forward possibly – out to Offiah and the left winger was away. Loughlin added the goal.

Test debutant Hugh Waddell made sufficient impression against France at Avignon to take the man-of-the-match award for his efforts in defence and his enthusiasm in taking the ball up in attack.

Hooker Kevin Beardmore, with his Castleford colleague, Kevin Ward, and Oldham's Hugh Waddell, formed an imposing front row in the Tests against France. Here Beardmore is held but looks to slip the ball out of the tackle.

There was almost certainly a forward pass involved in the next French score. But who would have begrudged Ratier his try as he streaked in from the right? Dumas added the goal points and the score was 14–18. Not for a long time had French enthusiasm been higher than it was at that moment. The final minutes, though, were dispiriting for them. Dixon, who had replaced Medley, burst through the French defence in midfield to create a chance which this time Hanley accepted decisively. Then, with the French attacking in the British '25', Schofield intercepted Dumas's pass and ran ninety yards for the touchdown. Pons chased him all the way but was never able to make any ground on the British centre. Creasser, who had taken Loughlin's place, added the goal points for Hanley's try but was unable to improve Schofield's.

France: Pougeau (St Estève); Ratier (Lézignan), Delaunay (St Estève), Fraisse (Le Pontet), Pons (St Gaudens); Espugna (Lézignan), Dumas (St Gaudens); Tisseyre (Pamiers), Khedimi (St Estève), Aillères (Toulouse), Montgaillard (XIII Catalan), Verdes (Villeneuve), Moliner (Lézignan)

Substitutes: Bienes (St Gaudens) for Fraisse after 50 minutes, Gestas (St Gaudens) for Moliner after 66 minutes

Scorers: tries – Verdes, Ratier; goals – Dumas (3)

Great Britain: Hampson (Wigan); Drummond (Warrington), Schofield (Leeds), Loughlin (St Helens), Offiah (Widnes); Hanley (Wigan), Edwards (Wigan); Ward (Castleford), Kevin Beardmore (Castleford), Waddell (Oldham), Powell (Leeds), Medley (Leeds), Platt (St Helens)

Substitutes: Dixon (Halifax) for Medley after 65 minutes, Creasser (Leeds) for Loughlin after 71 minutes

Scorers: tries – Schofield (2), Drummond, Offiah, Hanley; goals – Loughlin (3), Creasser

Referee: N. Kesha (New Zealand)

Attendance: 6,000

Headingley, Leeds, 6 February	**Great Britain 30 France 12**

Malcolm Reilly's most controversial decision for the return Whitbread Test at Headingley was to leave out Martin Offiah. Reilly euphemistically insisted that he had not been dropped: that it was still necessary at this stage to experiment. But it remained a contentious decision, suggesting perhaps that Offiah had already been discounted as a possible tourist.

But his omission was scarcely less surprising than France's decision to break up the Dumas–Espugna partnership with Frederic Bourrel coming in at scrum-half. Much less contentious was the replacement in the centre of the experienced Philippe Fourquet for David Fraisse, a 19-year-old who had looked out of his depth in Avignon. The pack was altered to let in Phillippe Gestas at loose forward with Moliner dropping to the bench.

Britain's other changes, apart from Plange for Offiah, saw Hanley moving from stand-off to centre in place of Loughlin; Gregory, who had been injured and unavailable for Avignon, resuming at scrum-half, with Edwards switching to stand-off; Ford replacing Drummond; Dixon coming into the second row for his first full Test and Medley occupying the bench where he was joined by his Leeds colleague, David Stephenson.

The objectives for Reilly's men were fairly obvious: tighten the defence, control the ball more and reduce the unforced errors. They were successful to a degree but while these improvements satisfied the British management the game offered the spectators nothing like the entertainment of Avignon and for the most part was watched in near silence. Even so, there were seven tries for a crowd of 7,000 to enjoy.

Steve Hampson at full-back emerged with the British man-of-the-match award, due recognition for a spirited performance. But while few reputations suffered any serious damage few, either, were enhanced. David Plange, on debut, scored a try and always looked determined but Phil Ford on the other wing received even fewer opportunities to display his elusive running. The recalled Fourquet was adjudged France's man-of-the-match but possibly a worthier candidate would have been Mathieu Khedimi, the hooker, who scored a try, made another, competed on almost equal terms with Kevin Beardmore at the scrums and whose mobility in broken play caused Britain some of their biggest problems.

Shaun Edwards, whose international season was severely curtailed by injury, on the bench at Headingley, after being forced to retire from the match against France. Alongside are Malcolm Reilly, the team manager Les Bettinson, and physiotherapist Geoff Plummer.

When Great Britain scored two tries in the opening four minutes memories of other French drubbings were inevitably recalled. On their two previous visits to Leeds they conceded more than 50 points each time. There was no capitulation on this occasion, however, even though the margin of defeat was conclusive enough. Gregory opened the scoring, gliding away from would-be pursuers after his little dummy close to the French line had caught the defence wrong-footed. Hanley scored the first of his two tries soon afterwards and then, on the half hour, played a central role in Schofield's fifteenth try in seventeen Tests. The French replied through Pons, the most important ingredient of a move, which also involved Espugna and Verdes, being a pass whipped out under pressure by Khedimi to his left winger.

Hanley's second try showed the strength of the man with Fourquet bouncing off him like a flyweight as he dashed for the line; and Plange's try, too, was well taken and executed with Gregory, Beardmore and Dixon combining and Schofield dexterously slipping the try-scoring pass off his hip.

The last try, with the admirable Khedimi galloping clear, was worth seeing for the jubilatory effect it had upon the French team and coach, Jorda, who had never strayed far from the touchline all afternoon as he exhorted his men to greater effort. If a slightly irrelevant try could mean so much to the French what might a victory over Britain, Australia or New Zealand do for their morale?

Great Britain: Hampson (Wigan); Plange (Castleford), Schofield (Leeds), Hanley (Wigan), Ford (Bradford Northern); Edwards (Wigan), Gregory (Wigan); Ward (Castleford), Kevin Beardmore (Castleford), Waddell (Oldham), Powell (Leeds), Dixon (Halifax), Platt (St Helens)

Substitutes: Medley (Leeds) for Powell after 60 minutes, Stephenson (Leeds) for Edwards after 72 minutes

Scorers: tries – Gregory, Hanley (2), Schofield, Plange; goals – Schofield (5)

France: Pougeau (St Estève); Ratier (Lézignan), Fourquet (St Gaudens), Delaunay (St Estève), Pons (St Gaudens); Espugna (Lézignan), Bourrel (Limoux); Tisseyre (Pamiers), Khedimi (St Estève), Aillères (Toulouse), Montgaillard (XIII Catalan), Verdes (Villeneuve), Gestas (St Gaudens)

Substitutes: Moliner (Lézignan) for Aillères after 52 minutes, Bienes (St Gaudens) not used

Scorers: tries – Pons, Khedimi; goals – Bourrel (2)

Referee: N. Kesha (New Zealand)

Attendance: 7,007

THE PAPUA NEW GUINEA TOUR

The tour by Papua New Guinea, known as the Kumuls (Birds of Paradise), had been eagerly awaited. They were expected to bring an exotic dash to the early part of the season; advance reports suggested that they had improved considerably since they had made a strictly amateur tour in 1979 and a marvellous victory over New Zealand, their first in any Tests, had done much for their credibility.

They were under the charge of an Australian coach, Barry Wilson, and their opening two matches were decidedly encouraging. In the first, against one of the best second division sides, Featherstone Rovers, they won 22–16, showing vulnerability on defence but some delightful attacking ideas also. An even better performance followed against Lancashire at St Helens where Bal Munapo, the tourists' captain, brought the scores level at 22–22 with the last kick of the game. It would have been an injustice if the Kumuls had lost after playing so much exhilarating rugby in which swift running, clever handling

19

and tackling of textbook correctness were the features. They led 20–10 at one stage but, still attempting to adapt to the conditions in the northern hemisphere, tired over the final stages during which sheer doggedness helped to take Lancashire into the lead at 22–20. Numapo's late penalty earned a deserved draw and all the pre-tour eulogies of the Kumuls' qualities appeared to be justified.

The next two games, against Swinton at Station Road (6–13) and Cumbria at Whitehaven (4–22), brought defeats for the Kumuls and some of the earlier optimism evaporated. Even so, the Whitbread Test four days after Whitehaven promised an awkward game for Britain. Certainly, the British management team had done their utmost to ensure that no trace of complacency had crept into the camp. At the end of a heavy (0–42) defeat, however, a desperately disappointed Barry Wilson was left to try to explain the inexplicable: why had a team of such obvious natural ability, of such instinctive flair and good habits, fallen so dismally short of expectations? Whatever the reason the Kumuls, before a crowd of 9,121 at Wigan's Central Park, 'froze' almost to the point of petrification. They never fully recovered from the disappointment. Three days later at Headingly, before a crowd (if so it could be described) of 1,780 they were heavily beaten by a Yorkshire side for whom Carl Gibson scored three tries; and in the final two matches in England they had only 4 points to spare in beating a Great Britain amateur side (20–16) and 8 in defeating Fulham (12–4).

The Kumuls' results in France suggested that they never did dispel the depression that descended upon them at Wigan. They enjoyed a sizable win over a Tarn selection (48–4), drew 12–12 with a Midi-Pyrenees selection but were beaten 14–18 by XIII Catalan and lost to France 4–21 in the Test at Carcassonne, where Fraisse scored two tries, Pons and Ratier getting the others. Kovae, from a superbly worked move, scored the Kumuls' one try.

Central Park,
Wigan,
24 October

Great Britain 42 Papua New Guinea 0
The most obsessive part of the British game plan in the Whitbread Test at Central Park was to try to prevent Papua New Guinea from scoring a try, and so faithfully did they follow the script that they prevented them from scoring any points at all. Even Australia, who had run in 62 points against the Kumuls at Port Moresby the year before, had not managed that; indeed in their twelve Tests to this stage the Kumuls had never failed to score a point. So for the British there was satisfaction to be had from knowing that a job had been efficiently executed. But for the spectators the match was a disappointment, largely because Papua never revealed their true attacking nature.

When they moved the ball along the line it was done at such a laboured pace that there was never the remotest chance they would open up the British defence as, for example, they had opened up Lancashire's. Their own defence meanwhile was pierced seven times and probably would have suffered even greater damage had Britain abandoned a strictly methodical style and thrown the ball about more – but that was not part of the script.

The game carried two World Cup points and these had been as good as secured by Britain after fifteen minutes with tries from Ford and Hanley. Hanley, incidentally, was playing at loose forward, thus becoming one of a rare

In the Test against Papua New Guinea at Central Park, Wigan, Andy Gregory steps out of a tackle on his way to scoring one of Great Britain's seven tries.

species to play in four different positions in a Test team. He was also one of eight Wigan players in the side – the most one club had contributed to a Great Britain side for thirty-seven years when Wigan again were the suppliers.

At the beginning of the second half Lomutopa came within inches of reaching the try-line and Krewanty made one highly dangerous run. But these forays amounted to little more than gestures . . . and reminders of the attacking flair of the Kumuls. Hampson, after looking defensively suspect the previous week playing for Lancashire, enjoyed a promising first appearance for Great Britain at full-back; so too did Paul Medley, the Leeds second-row forward. He was replaced by Karl Fairbank in the sixty-fifth minute but had done enough by then to earn himself the man-of-the-match award. Edwards controlled the midfield and in addition to his organisational prowess scored two tries. With Lydon, Hanley and Gregory also scoring tries and David Stephenson adding the goal points to each one, 34 of Britain's points came from Wigan players.

Great Britain: Hampson (Wigan); Drummond (Warrington), Stephenson (Wigan), Lydon (Wigan), Ford (Bradford Northern); Edwards (Wigan), Gregory (Wigan); Ward (Castleford), Groves (St Helens), Case (Wigan), Goodway (Wigan), Medley (Leeds), Hanley (Wigan)

Substitutes: Woods (Warrington) for Lydon and Fairbank (Bradford Northern) for Medley after 65 minutes

Scorers: tries – Edwards (2), Ford, Hanley, Medley, Lydon, Gregory; goals – Stephenson (7)

Papua New Guinea: Kovae; Krewanty, Atoi, Numapo, Saea; Haili, Kila; Tep, Heni, Lomutopa, Kombra, Waketsi, Taumaku

Substitutes: Kitimun for Haili after 55 minutes, Gaius for Kombra after 70 minutes

Referee: F. Desplas (France)

Attendance: 9,121

THE AUCKLAND TOUR

As with Papua New Guinea, Auckland, in some quarters at least, arrived to a sense of expectancy. But their six-match tour proved little more than a sideshow, and a slightly tatty one at that. This was a shame because there were many high-class players in the twenty-six-man squad and the side were capable of playing winning football. But Auckland did not always help their own cause. Their form was a curious mix, sometimes very good, indifferent at others, and running through their game was a streak of ill-discipline which possibly cost them potential customers.

It is possible that Auckland were also too obsessed with winning one game . . . against Wigan, whom they regarded as the best club side in the world, a legitimate estimate after Wigan's victory over Manly in the unofficial world club championship. They achieved that objective and felt that that result alone was vindication of their tour . . . a narrow view arguably. But the showpiece game, a match against the Chairman's XIII at Leeds, was a huge disappointment, watched by only 2,698 spectators.

Such a small gathering was not entirely unexpected. After winning their first two games against Leeds (29–25) and Warrington (22–16) Auckland were thrashed 26–52 by St Helens and an even more surprising defeat followed against Hull at the Boulevard. The lowest crowd there for more than a decade saw the tourists beaten 24–26 after they had looked to be in an impregnable position at half-time when they led 16–6. That was followed by their prestigious win 10–6 over Wigan but the damage had been done, and the victory arrived too late to generate other than tepid interest in the match against the Chairman's side.

Headingley, Leeds, 10 November

Chairman's XIII 12 Auckland 6
Tries from Martin Offiah and Phil Ford were enough to give the Chairman's XIII victory, Shane Horo's try in reply coming too late for Auckland. It was scored while the home side were reduced to eleven men with Lee Crooks sent off and Shaun Edwards spending ten minutes in the sin-bin. Peter Brown, the Auckland prop, had also been dismissed after the bout of fisticuffs with Crooks and so the violence which had marked the start of the tour against Leeds on the same ground was sadly in evidence at the end as well. When one recalled some of the outstanding rugby Auckland had produced to beat Warrington, for example, the tour seemed to have been a wasted opportunity to promote the best things in the sport.

Until this loss of temper midway through the second half the contest had barely generated enough therms to have heated an electric blanket. The British management had paid the contest due respect, treating it as an unofficial Test, but it could have told Malcolm Reilly, the British coach, little that he did not know already. Offiah, playing in his first representative match, made the most original of openings to the game, fielding the ball from the kick-off in the left corner and then running from one side of the field to the other, fractionally into the in-goal area at one point. But that slice of eccentricity was followed by an authentic piece of finishing in the nineteenth minute when he hurtled on to Edward's pass and outstripped a bewildered Auckland defence.

A try and a goal soon after the interval effectively settled the contest. A high, searching kick by Fox troubled John Ropati. He failed to gather the ball, Ford took full advantage of the blunder, scored close to the posts and Whitfield was left to kick his second easy goal of the night.

The Auckland tourists included some talented individuals, among them their winger, Shane Horo, seen here in attack in their much-prized victory over Wigan.

Chairman's XIII: John Myler (Widnes); Ford (Bradford Northern), Schofield (Leeds), Whitfield (Halifax), Offiah (Widnes); Edwards (Wigan), Fox (Featherstone Rovers); Crooks (Leeds), McCallion (Halifax), Powell (Leeds), Fairbank (Bradford Northern), Roberts (Warrington), Platt (St Helens)

Substitutes: Dixon (Halifax) for Roberts after 59 minutes, Forster (Warrington) not used

Scorers: tries – Offiah, Ford; goals – Whitfield (2)

23

Auckland: John Ropati; Panapa, Tea Ropati, Tuimavave, Shane Horo; Cooper, Freeman; Brown, Hooker, Goulding, Kaiser, Peter Ropati, Mark Horo.

Substitutes: Patton for Tuimavave after 60 minutes, Crequer not used

Scorers: try – Shane Horo; goal – Brown

Referee: J. Holdsworth (Kippax)

Attendance: 2,698

WIGAN v. MANLY

Central Park, Wigan, 7 October

Wigan 8 Manly 2

The night Wigan beat Manly for the unofficial world club championship will retain an imperishable place in the memories of the 36,895 spectators at Central Park. The atmosphere crackled with excitement and expectation and the sides responded with a contest that was as raw as red meat, but skilful too, and utterly absorbing. Wigan's vision in arranging such a game was amply rewarded. It proved a sizable financial success as well as giving the club in particular and the game in general much prestige. It was a win, too, made the more significant for being achieved without an overseas player in the Wigan team. The overriding theme afterwards was that the experiment must be repeated and if the proposed official world club championship in Japan in 1989 comes to fruition then Wigan will take their share of the credit.

Such a contest always had the potential to capture the public's imagination, but no one could quite have foreseen the scale of it. But here was a good example of the benefits to be gained when a saleable product is marketed in the right way. The pity was that it was ignored by the television companies. Unusually for Rugby League there were no tries, but television had wasted the chance to show the game at its compelling best. Manly, who had earned the right to play Wigan by virtue of their victory over Canberra in Sydney's Grand Final, were provided with plenty of financial inducement to win the game – a winner-take-all prize of £20,000 that would have given the players useful spending money as they returned to Australia via a holiday in Honolulu.

To achieve this win Wigan needed to be at their most accomplished in an area of the game where Australians are often superior to English players – in defence. Wigan's success of the previous season, when they had won four of the five major trophies available to them, had been due significantly to the security of their defence, which then proved the launching pad for a succession of devastating counter-attacks. The quality of their defence was now put to one of its severest tests and it was not found lacking. Over the final stages, when the excitement reached fever pitch and it gradually dawned on Manly that they might not win, the Wigan line had to absorb some ferocious onslaughts. It held nobly.

Both sides were clearly highly motivated and the opening exchanges were excessively physical, with Michael O'Connor, the classiest of centres, and

Ellery Hanley of Wigan and Manly's Paul Shaw in the unofficial world club challenge match, which was not only one of the great Rugby League contests of this or any other season but which marked the start of an official world club challenge.

David Stephenson exchanging penalties to put the sides level at 2–2. The undercurrent of violence never entirely left the contest. In the first half there was a brawl and Cliff Lyons was sent to the sin-bin; while in the second Ron Gibbs was sent off after a late challenge which poleaxed Joe Lydon. But it will be the pace of the game, the skill under intense pressure, and the sheer physical commitment that will be remembered.

Wigan benefited most from the ill-discipline with Stephenson landing two penalties before half time and another two after it. It was hard to see Wigan coming by points in any other way against an impregnable Manly defence. But then Manly could find no way through Wigan's defence either.

Wigan: Hampson; Russell, Stephenson, Lydon, Gill; Edwards, Gregory; Case, Kiss, Wane, Goodway, Potter, Hanley

Substitutes: Byrne, West, Lucas, Gildart

Scorer: goals – Stephenson (4)

Manly: Shearer; Ronson, Williams, O'Connor, Davis; Lyons, Hasler; Daley, Cochrane, Gately, Gibbs, Cunningham, Vautin

Substitutes: Brokenshire, Ticehurst, Pocock, Shaw

Scorer: goal – O'Connor

Referee: J. Holdsworth (Kippax)

Attendance: 36,895

UNDER-21 AND COLTS INTERNATIONALS

In addition to their two open-age internationals, Great Britain and France played each other at Under-21 and Colts levels, home and away, with the following results:

Salon,
23 January

France Juniors 10 Great Britain Colts 17

France Juniors: Etienne (Roanne); J.-M. Bourrel (Limoux), Nadalin (Albi), Vergniol (Villeneuve), Toniol (Toulouse); Foulquier (Limoux), Mas (Entraigues); Quillien (Carpentras), Giudicelli (Albi), Costes (Carcassonne), Alibert (Albi), Cabestany (St Estève), Amat (Carcassonne)

Substitutes: Luchese (Aussillon), Ascencio (Carcassonne), Crismanowich (Châtillon)

Scorers: tries – Mas, Toniol; goal – Vergniol

Great Britain Colts: Longstaff (Halifax); Sullivan (Hull KR), Richard Price (Hull), Anderson (Castleford), Farrell (Huddersfield); Irwin (Castleford), Delaney (Leeds); Neil (St Helens), Jackson (Hull), Hill (Castleford), Gildart (Wigan), Betts (Wigan), Gary Price (Wakefield Trinity)

Substitutes: Roebuck (Bradford Northern), Butt (Leeds), Amann (Leeds), Nolan (Hull)

Scorers: tries – Gary Price, Betts, Hill; goals – Longstaff, Roebuck; drop-goal – Hill

Aussillon,
6 March

France Espoirs 14 Great Britain Under-21 13

France Espoirs: Frison (Toulouse); Toniol (Toulouse), Vergniol (Villeneuve), Fraisse (Le Pontet), Pougeau (St Estève); Espugna (Lézignan), Zenon (Châtillon); Mimouni (Pia), Valero (Lézignan), Grandjean (Lézignan), Divet (Limoux), Blachère (Le Pontet), Moliner (Lézignan)

Substitutes: F. Bourrel (Limoux), Bardes (St Estève)

Scorers: tries – Divet, Fraisse; goals – Fraisse, Pougeau, Grandjean

Great Britain Under-21: Lord (Castleford); Pratt (Leeds), Fletcher (Hull KR), Wright (Widnes), Johnson (Leeds); Irwin (Castleford), Parker (Hull KR); Lucas (Wigan), Dermott (Wigan), Hill (Castleford), Gildart (Wigan), Sampson (Castleford), Sanderson (Warrington)

Substitutes: Cassidy (Swinton), Harmon (Warrington)

Scorers: tries – Sampson, Pratt; goals – Fletcher (2); drop-goal – Parker
26

Knowsley Road, **Great Britain Colts 18 France Juniors 6**
St Helens,
19 March

Great Britain Colts: Longstaff (Halifax); Phil Price (St Helens), Richard Price (Hull), Anderson (Castleford), Farrell (Huddersfield); Irwin (Castleford), Delaney (Leeds); Neil (St Helens), Jackson (Hull), Amann (Leeds), Nolan (Hull), Betts (Wigan), Roebuck (Bradford Northern)

Substitutes: Fawcett (Leeds), Butt (Leeds), Forshaw (Wigan), Ball (Wigan)

Scorers: tries – Farrell, Delaney, Irwin, Anderson; goal – Longstaff

France Juniors: Simon (Limoux); Reyre (Avignon), Vergniol (Villeneuve), Foulquier (Limoux), Foual (Le Pontet); Crismanowich (Châtillon), Mas (Entraigues); Quillien (Carpentras), Ascencio (Carcassonne), Boyer (Villeneuve), Cabestany (St Estève), Jammes (Limoux), Amat (Carcassonne)

Substitutes: Costes (Carcassonne), Luchese (Aussillon), Hourcault (Villeneuve)

Scorers: try – Vergniol; goal – Crismanowich

Knowsley Road, **Great Britain Under-21 4 France Espoirs 8**
St Helens,
19 March

Great Britain Under-21: Bibb (Featherstone R.); Pratt (Leeds), Fletcher (Hull KR), Cassidy (Swinton), Johnson (Leeds); Robinson (Halifax), Parker (Hull KR); Lucas (Wigan), Dermott (Wigan), Hill (Castleford), Gildart (Wigan), Harmon (Warrington), Sanderson (Warrington)

Substitutes: Russell (Wigan), Price (Wakefield Trinity)

Scorers: goals – Fletcher (2)

France Espoirs: Frison (Toulouse); Chiron (Carpentras), Pougeau (St Estève), Fraisse (Le Pontet), Carrière (Lézignan); Espugna (Lézignan), Zenon (Châtillon); Mimouni (Pia), Valero (Lézignan), Grandjean (Lézignan), Blachère (Le Pontet), Divet (Limoux), Pech (Limoux)

Substitutes: Martial (Châtillon), Bardes (St Estève)

Scorers: try – Espugna; goals – Fraisse (2)

TWO

The Stones Bitter Championship and Premiership Trophies

Trevor Watson

THE STONES BITTER CHAMPIONSHIP

Widnes timed things to perfection, saving the best until the last, as they clinched the Stones Bitter Championship for the first time for ten years in their final fixture. The triumph was completed in style, a 66–14 romp at Hunslet, and earned the Chemics £20,000. It left their chief rivals, St Helens and Wigan, each with two games remaining, competing for the runners-up spot and £9,000, Saints taking the minor honours on points difference.

Widnes were in command for much of the season and led the table almost throughout. They were overtaken for a matter of three days by St Helens on the run-in, but an emphatic win at Warrington, followed by a crucial success over Saints, when winger Martin Offiah scored all their three tries to make certain of his tour place, ensured that only a major disaster at Hunslet would prevent the title going to Naughton Park. Weakened Hunslet, booked for relegation, discovered the gap that exists in the first division and conceded twelve tries.

It was a notable achievement by Widnes, who played most of the season without their injured stand-off, Tony Myler. He played at Hunslet but then had to go into hospital for a knee operation as his year ended sadly. There was the skilled presence of the Australian Dale Shearer, to atone for Myler's absence for a time, but as so often in the past their strength lay in their ability to find players to slot in and do a sound job. The side was superbly balanced, led by that vastly influential forward Kurt Sorensen. There was a marvellous link with his hooker, Phil McKenzie, whose speed in the open enabled him to set up a number of victories.

Well aware of the need for strength in depth in the forwards, Widnes signed Derek Pyke from Leigh and the New Zealander Joe Grima from Swinton during the season to ensure that they had ample cover in the later matches when, so often, teams are caught napping by injuries. Widnes also emerged with the find of the season in Martin Offiah, whose searing pace provided them with that extra cutting edge which the graft of the men inside him needed. Offiah's try-scoring feats, including breaking the club record of thirty-four held by Frank Myler, tended to overshadow some rapid late improvement by Andy Currier, who made a great success of being introduced at centre and scored some valuable tries, including four in a resounding win at Castleford.

David Hulme's gritty performances throughout the season earned him a tour spot and their loose forward, Richard Eyres, was perhaps unlucky not to be given more credit for his efforts. The O'Neill brothers, Mike and Steve, also played their parts and full-back John Myler was unfortunate that a series of sound displays was forgotten by many outsiders after a couple of televised errors were highlighted. He deserved better.

Widnes were off to the right sort of start with six successive wins and after a startling upset at home to Swinton – the first win of the season by the Lions – they registered another six victories to move into the new year in a very favourable position. They overcame a crushing 0–25 defeat by in-form St Helens at Knowsley Road early in the new year, and their only real worries arrived when they lost at home to Wigan and then surprisingly at Hull KR. They also crashed heavily again in the away fixture at Wigan but between times had crushed the Yorkshire challenge of Leeds, when Offiah collected a hat-trick of tries, and Castleford to keep their hopes very much alive.

Wigan then stepped in to do Widnes an important favour by winning at St Helens on Good Friday to put the title at stake in the Widnes v. St Helens match at Naughton Park on Easter Monday. Offiah's hat-trick in that game settled matters and the win at Hunslet was little more than a formality. The Saints' programme later carried three tributes to Offiah: one writer describing him as the difference between the sides – praise indeed.

For some time, St Helens, with matches in hand, appeared capable of finishing at the top of the table. In an astonishing spell they amassed 64 points against Hull, 70 against luckless Hunslet and 50 at Leigh to underline their challenge. But those cricket scores came when their Kiwi stand-off, Shane Cooper, was at Knowsley Road. Just how important he was became all-too apparent when he returned to New Zealand. He was irreplaceable.

There was no doubting the highlight of the St Helens league season: their remarkable win at Wigan over Christmas. They trailed 6–22 at the interval, yet fought back to win 32–22, their full-back, Phil Veivers, scoring two tries and Paul Loughlin landing six goals. Their prop-forward, Tony Burke, produced some strong displays and Roy Haggerty's performances pushed him into the tour squad, while hooker Paul Groves, another tourist, proved an excellent signing from Salford. There was also the recruitment of the heavyweight prop, Stuart Evans from Neath Rugby Union, to beef up the pack. But a deal with another Welsh RU star, the scrum-half David Bishop, fell through at the last moment, apparently on medical grounds.

Loose forward Andy Platt's wholehearted tackling and high work-rate earned him tour selection, although he ended the season on the transfer list. Injuries kept the wing signing, Les Quirk, the forward John Fieldhouse, and the half-back, Neil Holding, on the sidelines for lengthy spells and left the squad a shade under strength.

Wigan began as firm title favourites but their involvement in too many knock-out competitions and representative demands on so many players took a toll. Despite the upset against St Helens, the Central Park men were still very much a title threat and it's perhaps more than a coincidence that things really went wrong after they had qualified for Wembley. Then Wigan lost at home to Warrington and away to Hull and Hull KR in the space of eight days and the championship had gone, yet they took full points from Widnes, which is some consolation. The loss of their New Zealand Test centre, Dean Bell, for much of the season was a heavy blow, despite the excellent form shown by another Kiwi, the teenager Kevin Iro, and his brother Tony on the wing.

Bell's defensive strength and attacking experience were hard to replace and matters were not helped with Henderson Gill and Joe Lydon on the injury list for some time. However, great service was given by the half-backs, Shaun Edwards and Andy Gregory. Edwards thrived on being named captain, while Gregory adopted a far less abrasive approach and looked all the better for it. Some of their chip-kick moves with their brilliant full-back, Steve Hampson, were a joy to watch. Hampson became the outstanding full-back in the country by some distance and never knew how to ease off; his attacking work was a delight.

Though he ended the season on the transfer-list, Andy Platt's wholehearted tackling and high work-rate for St Helens earned him selection for the Lions' tour of Australasia. After an injured ankle delayed his start, he acquitted himself with great credit, especially in the match against Manly, where he was easily the pick of the pack. Sadly, a broken wrist meant an early return to Britain.

The prop-forward, Brian Case, shirked nothing and combined well with hooker Nicky Kiss. Andy Goodway was devastating on occasions and Graeme West revelled in a return to senior action whenever he played. The dispute between the coach, Graham Lowe, and Ellery Hanley hit the headlines but did not affect team spirit. Hanley, to his credit, returned to produce some match-winning performances, notably an outstanding display under extreme pressure at St Helens.

Bradford Northern finished fourth and were always a difficult team to beat with their big and businesslike pack. Heavyweight Brendan Hill and his fellow

30

prop Kelvin Skerrett played important roles, fitting in well with the experienced David Hobbs and Brian Noble. They covered for the loss of veteran Jeff Grayshon, who broke a leg in the autumn but still bounced back towards the end of the season. Their form was so good that it was some surprise that their strong-running second-row forward, Karl Fairbank, was the only Odsal forward to gain selection in the original tour squad. Northern were organised magnificently by their scrum-half, Paul Harkin; the full-back, Keith Mumby, was again totally reliable, while their winger, Phil Ford, scored some magical tries. Northern signed two little-known New Zealanders, Gary Mercer and Russell Stewart, and they proved good acquisitions. Mercer in particular made an impact with his keen tackling and straight running to collect thirteen tries in his short stay. The one problem for Bradford was that spectators did not like Odsal, with its one stand partly exposed and a marked lack of atmosphere. Nine of their twelve league games there had attendances below 5,000, two of them less than 3,000. A crowd of 11,310 for the match against Wigan at Bradford City's Valley Parade gave rise to speculation regarding ground-sharing.

Leeds, shaken by a brush with relegation the previous season, responded in typical fashion with a massive spending spree. They twice smashed the world record, paying £172,500 for Lee Crooks and £178,250 for Garry Schofield, both from Hull. Other signings were John Basnett, from Widnes, Alan Rathbone, from Warrington, Gary Spencer and John Lyons in a complex exchange and cash deal with Wakefield Trinity, and David Stephenson, from Wigan. They recruited the Australians Peter Tunks, Peter Jackson, Steve Morris and Marty Gurr, and the New Zealand All Black forward, Mark Brooke-Cowden. For good measure they also signed the amateur international, John Fairbank; their overall deals were estimated at £700,000. Results were mixed with no

Lee Crooks joined Leeds from Hull at the beginning of the season for £172,500 but, affected by serious injury, played only ten full games for his new club.

trophies to show but attendances at Headingley regularly topped 10,000 for the first time for almost thirty years and some superb rugby was played.

Crooks, however, played only ten full games because of injury, and Spencer eight, while Rathbone lasted a mere thirteen minutes. That magnificent runner Paul Medley also had a much-reduced season. Schofield and Carl Gibson became the first to score twenty tries in a season for Leeds for an astonishing eight years, big-hearted Roy Powell had an excellent season and there was good work too from Gurr and Dave Heron. But the departure of the three other Australians before the end of February left a big gap and title hopes, strong at one stage, faded with some away lapses.

Other clubs never figured in the title hunt. Warrington had their moments but slipped out of the top four as injuries bit. They did well to figure at all after early injuries forced them to play makeshift teams. That soothing personality Les Boyd twice broke an arm, the second time in February, which ended his career. Their scrum-half, Keith Holden, a £10,000 bargain from Wigan, played well but missed the last two months to wreck his tour hopes, and Des Drummond was another casualty on the injury list for a long while. There were flashes of inspiration from stand-off John Woods, who continued to pile up the points with his goalkicking and Gary Sanderson and Billy McGinty impressed up front.

Castleford were disappointed with the form of their Australian recruits, Bob Lindner, Michael Beattie and John Fifita. Their international, Lindner, in particular, was well below par, missing many matches; on his return to Sydney he indulged in some spiteful criticism of the club, who sharply attacked his attitude to training and playing. Kevin Ward impressed in patches but his fellow prop, Barry Johnson, felt the effects of being out injured until February. It was left to their old hand, John Joyner, to show consistency; David Roockley worked well at full-back and their teenage half-back, Shaun Irwin maintained his promise.

Halifax had a moderate league season and only five wins from their first fifteen matches put them among the relegation candidates. However, one of those wins was at Wigan to end the Central Park club's winning run of twenty-nine matches. There was a mid-season improvement but they too suffered from lapses of concentration when Wembley beckoned. Graham Eadie returned for another season and was named as the new coach when Chris Anderson confirmed his move back to Australia. Among the usual strong Aussie contingent was Bob Grogan, who, after a quiet start, became a very good stand-off, teaming up well with the young scrum-half, Steve Robinson.

The fast-running centre, Tony Anderson, came back after a knee operation to get among the tries but the main Thrum Hall strength was up front, where the prop, Keith Neller, had a fine season and Paul Dixon's powerful running earned tour selection. The club achieved another shrewd signing in Les Holliday, from Swinton, who became a commanding figure and played a significant part in the Cup run.

It was a season to forget on Humberside. Both Hull Kingston Rovers and Hull missed the top eight; neither had a big enough squad to cope with the challenge for the premiership and recruiting was limited. Rovers were kept alive by their good home form, the work of half-back Wayne Parker and the

Phil Ford scored some memorable tries for Bradford Northern in helping them to fourth place in the championship and well deserved his selection for the Lions' tour of Australasia, where he played consistently well at full-back, centre or on the wing.

steady goalkicking of Mike Fletcher, while Zook Ema was consistent up front.

Hull, of course, lost key men with the sale of Crooks and Schofield and had some bad moments until four successive wins eased relegation fears. Their stand-off, Gary Pearce, sparkled on occasions and the Boulevarders owed much to the Australian second-row pair, Terry Regan and David Brooks, for providing essential graft and to their half-back, Paul McCaffery, for some lively work when the pressure was on.

No one was surprised at the prompt return to the second division of Hunslet and Swinton. They did not strengthen their squads sufficiently to cope with the higher division, although Hunslet were unfortunate that two of their three Australians, stand-off Trevor Benson and half-back Mark Hohn, played only a handful of games. The third Aussie, the second-row forward, David Gillespie, worked hard in a lost cause, but much of the season was in the hands of youngsters. One of these, the back-row forward, Sonny Nickle, made a tremendous impact before being injured and Steve Lay earned his spurs at full-back.

Swinton, like Hunslet, found the all-round pace in the first division too demanding and the departure of Holliday didn't help their cause. There was good service later on from a new signing, Tommy Frodsham, at stand-off.

With two clubs condemned early, a keen struggle developed to avoid the last relegation place and it came down to Salford and Leigh, with the issue decided on the last day. Salford, two points ahead, even went to the trouble of putting back their kick-off against Halifax to prevent Leigh having a half-hour advantage. The precaution was unnecessary. Salford beat Halifax comfortably before their biggest League crowd of the season, 6,716, so Leigh's win over Hull was in vain. Maybe Salford deserved to survive once again if only for their enterprise in signing the Australian Test star, Garry Jack, and the England Rugby Union international, Peter Williams. Jack played only briefly but certainly brightened the scene and, on his departure, his fellow Australian, Steve Gibson, stepped in and became a folk hero at the Willows with some thrilling displays, highlighted by a hat-trick of tries in a home win over Leigh that proved crucial. Williams, a stand-off from Orrell, played at centre and scored a try on his debut in the win over Leigh. He collected five tries in as many matches to help save his club and come, remarkably, into tour reckoning.

When Halifax signed Les Holliday from Swinton they obtained an experienced forward who developed into a commanding figure and played impressively for them in both league and cup.

Relegation for Leigh was realisation of a fear that too often haunts them these days. They were not strong enough to compete regularly in the top bracket and a mid-season spell, enlivened by their New Zealander, Shane Horo, and some neat touches by Harry Pinner, was never enough.

The second division promotion teams were wholly predictable, the only question was whether Oldham, Wakefield Trinity or Featherstone Rovers would be champions. They took it in turns but on the penultimate weekend of the season Oldham won a thriller 23–22 at Wakefield to clinch the title, and a late run by Rovers earned second place.

After a difficult season Salford survived in the first division and deserved to do so if only because of their enterprise in signing the great Australian fullback, Garry Jack. Though he played comparatively few games his presence brought real quality to the Willows.

For a relegated team, Oldham invested heavily in new players, signing second-row forward, Paul Round, from St Helens, and later their scrum-half Mike Ford, who earned a place in the squad going to Australia. They had an impressive Rugby Union trialist, who signed soon after his name was leaked: New Zealander Charlie McAlister became a sizable and popular figure in the three-quarters. Prop Hugh Waddell's form gained him two international appearances and Oldham were gratified to find that fans kept faith after the previous season's relegation: attendances were very encouraging. Featherstone, under their new coach Peter Fox, lost four of their first eight matches. But once Fox had established a pattern they became very hard to beat and took seven points from their four games against Trinity and Oldham. Their mainspring was inevitably their scrum-half, Deryck Fox, who worked well with Graham Steadman, and with the evergreen forward Peter Smith, and organised magnificently a team that grew in confidence.

Wakefield Trinity appointed David Topliss as player-coach and, helped by the deal with Leeds, he strengthened the side, bringing centre Andy Mason, winger Phil Fox, half-back Mark Conway and the prop-forward Keith Rayne to Belle Vue. All did well, with Conway outstanding, and there was sound support from the hooker, Billy Conway, and versatile Nigel Bell. Trinity had the title in their grasp but four defeats in their last five games proved fatal.

Sheffield Eagles were enterprising under the guidance of Gary Hetherington and led the table for a time, having played more matches. They are frustrated in never having been drawn at home to a top team in order to test the local

35

public, although there was an interesting experiment with one home game being played at Sheffield United's Bramall Lane.

Another club trying a soccer venue was Springfield Borough, the new name for the old Blackpool club, who moved into the Wigan Athletic football ground at the beginning of the season. Led by the experienced Bob Eccles and with the young full-back, Mike Smith, coming good with his kicking, Springfield did well enough to finish fourth. However, attendances did not reflect the club's efforts and the hoped-for overspill from their giant Central Park neighbours never materialised.

There is good rugby to be seen in the lower division but unfortunately fans demand more glamour and the majority of clubs, hard hit by ground safety regulations, simply struggled along.

THE PREMIERSHIP TROPHIES

The Rugby Football League's decision again to stage the Stones Bitter Premiership finals as a 'double-header' at Old Trafford was thoroughly justified and provided an outstanding climax to the season. A crowd of 35,252 were thrilled by a classic second division final in which Oldham edged out Featherstone Rovers after an enthralling game and then admired the supreme professionalism and incisive finishing of the champions, Widnes, as they outplayed below-strength St Helens. The standard of play and holiday atmosphere among a crowd basking in glorious sunshine helped eliminate memories of the unpleasant Widnes v. Warrington semi-final the previous Sunday, which attracted the wrong sort of publicity for several days and had such dramatic repercussions.

The finals underlined once more that Rugby League has so much to offer as family entertainment and how spectacular are its big occasions. It was noticeable that the vast majority of the crowd were in their seats for the start of the second division game and all were there for the start of the second half. All 26,000 seats had been sold in advance, making it clear that fans expect comfort, especially on such a long day, and this helped towards record receipts for the Premiership of more than £200,000. Like it or not, soccer's stadiums have an important part to play in the promotion of Rugby League and the sporting spirit of the finals was happily emphasised when all the spectators rose to applaud the teams after their respective games in a spontaneous gesture of approval.

It was no great surprise that the Wembley finalists, Wigan and Halifax, should go out in the opening round of the Premiership, played just a week before the Challenge Cup final. Even though Wigan had home advantage, they were up against a Warrington side becoming used to winning at Central Park and in no mood to let a Cup-conscious team off the hook. John Woods played a crucial role for Warrington, landing six goals from seven attempts and he also created a try for David Lyon. But the incident which turned the game was a long-range interception try by Mark Forster. With Mike Gregory creating a score for Mark Roskell, Warrington eased home 24–12, their fourth win in their last six games against Wigan, another being a draw.

Halifax found the champions, Widnes, in buoyant mood and scrum-half David Hulme celebrated his tour selection with an enterprising two-try display. Widnes were coasting 24–8 at the interval. Although the Halifax forwards roused themselves in the second half to narrow the gap at one stage to 4 points, the Chemics eased clear again, with Martin Offiah scoring his forty-fourth try of the season.

The inspiration of that great Kiwi forward, Kurt Sorensen, was a major factor in Widnes's Championship and Premiership triumphs.

There was a dazzling eighty-yard touchdown by another tour winger, Phil Ford, who left the Leeds defence rooted as Bradford Northern comfortably beat the Headingley men for the fourth time in the season, 32–18. The second-row forward, David Hobbs, with six goals, and the heavyweight prop, Brendan Hill, who took the man-of-the-match award, again tried to show that their omission from the tour was a mistake with impressive displays.

In the remaining first division tie of that round, St Helens had little trouble in ending Castleford's season on a disappointing note, winning 40–8 at Knowsley Road. Their hooker, Paul Groves, was their star, collecting a hat-trick of tries in another of his lively displays in the loose.

The second division ties remained true to form, with the top four all reaching the semi-finals. The closest tie, again predictable, was at Springfield Borough, where the home men needed a late penalty-goal by Mike Smith for a win against Sheffield. The visitors scored two tries to one, both from Neil Kellett, but Smith's kicking saved the home team, not for the first time. The

37

match was played on the Sunday evening to avoid a clash with Wigan. The Central Park attendance was 15,926 while the turn-out for Springfield was 530.

Mal Graham and Kevin Meadows each collected two tries for Oldham in their 34–24 success over Keighley, who finished with a flourish to narrow the gap. The centre, Alan Banks, also touched down twice for Featherstone Rovers, who collected eight tries in the 44–1 romp against Mansfield.

Wakefield Trinity wobbled to trail 12–18 to York but they pulled away to win easily 44–23, Nigel Bell, Phil Eden and Steve Halliwell each scoring two tries. A feature of the first rounds was that three of the Fairbank brothers scored a try for different clubs. Second-row forward Karl for Bradford, prop Dick for Halifax and centre Mark for Keighley.

The semi-finals were totally and unhappily dominated by the ugly events at Naughton Park, another classic case of the game shooting itself firmly in the foot after all the good publicity from Wembley a week earlier. Pictures of a young boy being carried off after being knocked down by brawling players, who spilled over the touchline, appalled everyone. They were allied to stories of crowd violence, which caused police reinforcements to be called up, and Test star Des Drummond was alleged to have struck a spectator who had run on to the pitch. Within days Drummond felt the backlash as he was withdrawn from the Great Britain tour party along with Wigan's Joe Lydon, who had been involved in a Good Friday incident with a spectator at St Helens.

Some felt the two players had been pre-judged and their side of the story had not been heard. But those outside the code praised the League for their decisive action in seeking to restore the game's image at a difficult time. Yet amid all the bitterness and the brawling, there was good rugby to appreciate in the Widnes match. Warrington's stand-off, John Woods, gave them a marvellous start with a slick solo try and tacked on three goals to put his side 10–0 ahead. They held this healthy lead until the thirty-second minute, when a clever kick by Barry Dowd enabled winger Rick Thackray to gather and race away to score between the posts. Duncan Platt's goal trimmed the deficit to 4 points.

Within two minutes Widnes had taken charge and again a clever kick played a part. Their centre, Andy Currier, swooped to gather when Woods lost the ball. He kicked ahead, re-gathered and scored from forty yards. Platt's goal put the Chemics in front. Kurt Sorensen again set an inspiring lead as Widnes stayed in charge and they eased away with a try by David Hulme and two further goals by Platt. Widnes had a fright when Martin Offiah was taken off with a knee injury, though he was later given the all-clear after X-rays, while Warrington's centre, Paul Cullen, played on despite a broken arm. Sadly the memories for the 10,453 spectators were not of courage, skill or commitment, but of the ugly side of things after the scenes of violence on the terraces and on the field.

In the other semi-final, St Helens had a crowd of 10,461 for a keen-looking tie against Bradford Northern. Both teams were largely out of touch although the strength of the Odsal pack was in evidence once more, and Saints did well to keep them in check. Northern led 10–8 at the interval. A fine break and slick pass by Keith Mumby enabled Heath Godfrey to send in Steve McGowan for a try, and Hobbs landed three goals to four by Paul Loughlin.

However, Neil Holding turned matters early in the second half when he made one of his quick breaks and Andy Platt was at his shoulder to score the try. Loughlin's goal made it 14–10 to Saints. Hobbs went close for Northern but St Helens held out and finished in style with a sharp try by Groves. Loughlin added two more goals to make his tally seven from nine attempts and Roy Haggerty chipped in with two drop-goals to round off a good day for the St Helens tourists. Good, that is, until Platt discovered he had an injured ankle, which ruled him out of the final and delayed his departure for Australasia.

In the second division semi-finals, Featherstone Rovers were given a tough time by their neighbours, Wakefield Trinity, who scored after only two minutes at Post Office Road through Gary Haggerty. Then the half-backs, Graham Steadman and Deryck Fox, began to control matters behind a pack in which Paul Hughes was impressive. All three got on to the scoresheet and there was another try for the prop, Karl Harrison, to go with two goals by Steve Quinn, as Rovers held off a lively Trinity rally to win 20–16. Scrum-half Mark Conway had a magnificent game for Trinity, who scored further tries through Nigel Bell and Steve Halliwell with Conway landing two goals. They had Rovers worried at 10–10 early in the second half but in the end the result was right.

Springfield Borough won plenty of friends among a crowd of 4,667 at Oldham with a spirited performance. The game was in the balance for some time until 10 points in twelve minutes after the interval took Oldham clear. They were indebted to big Charlie McAlister for his matchwinning contribution of a try and three goals, other tries coming from Des Foy and Mal Graham.

Springfield's wholehearted efforts meant that Oldham couldn't relax until the end and Borough were by no means disgraced by the 10–19 scoreline as they rocked the champions with a try by Carl Briscoe and three goals by Mike Smith.

However, the scene was set for two cracking Premiership finals, the second division champions Oldham against Featherstone Rovers and the first division title winners Widnes against St Helens. It proved a marvellous occasion.

Old Trafford, Manchester, 15 May

The Second Division Premiership Trophy Final
Oldham 28 Featherstone Rovers 26
The scoreline said it all as Oldham and Featherstone Rovers proved beyond doubt that the second division has a rightful place on Premiership day. The game was played at high speed, with many spectacular moments. There was a devastating first thirty-two minutes by Oldham to lead 22–0, an incredible fight-back by Rovers to lead 26–22 before Oldham snatched the trophy at the end. Little wonder the crowd applauded both teams for minutes on end.

Oldham's Des Foy took the man-of-the-match award for some lightning breaks which brought him two tries and a major part in the winning try. But he was pressed all the way by Featherstone's Graham Steadman, who also scored two tries, and Steve Quinn, who gave an immaculate exhibition of goal-kicking to lift his side. Rovers were without their full-back, Chris Bibb, and moved Quinn from centre to No 1, while Oldham sprang a surprise, playing second-row forward, Paul Round, on the right wing.

Both sides soon showed their willingness to move the ball and Rovers went close when a good short pass from Keith Bell sent Paul Hughes tearing for the corner. Mick Burke used all his 15½ stone to make a timely tackle. Oldham's reply was smooth handling and Quinn had to make smart tackles on Mick Ford and Terry Flanagan in quick succession. Round missed a chance when he was unable to gather a bouncing pass from Des Foy with the line open, but it was only a temporary set-back as Flanagan's well-judged pass sent Foy racing over for Charlie McAlister to add the goal.

Oldham's Hugh Waddell, after passing out of the tackle, watches Dave Hawkyard, with Mal Graham in support, make the surge which led to the Lancashire club's third try in a fine passage of play in the second-division Premiership final.

That score set Oldham alight and they played some dazzling rugby. Burke came charging through and Kevin Meadows cut inside before slipping a neat pass to send Flanagan over. McAlister's kick failed but at 10–0 Oldham were buzzing. Their third try, after twenty-five minutes, was a marvellous piece of combined play between forwards and backs. Hugh Waddell made the drive, Dave Hawkyard supported to provide the vital break before finding Mal Graham, who held the ball nicely and sent Foy racing clear for the try after a seventy-yard sweep. McAlister's goal made it 16–0.

Rovers were unlucky when Paul Lyman pounced on a grubber kick by Deryck Fox but the try was disallowed, and Oldham hared out of defence through Flanagan, Graham and Foy. More slick handling, this time involving Meadows, Burke and Foy, saw Peter Walsh provide the final touch and McAlister's goal made it 22–0 and apparently all over. We should have known better. Just before the interval Rovers gained what looked like being their only consolation when Steadman sent out a long pass to David Sykes. The latter did well to keep the ball alive in a two-man tackle and slipped a pass back to Steadman, who went in at the corner. Quinn's goal made it 6–22.

The second half was astonishing. Early on Rovers brought on substitutes John Crossley and John Bastian for Gary Siddall and Richard Marsh. Crossley went to stand-off with Steadman at centre and Sykes on the wing. Things became interesting when Steadman scored again. This time he chipped ahead and won the race as the ball bounced over the line for a picture try to which Quinn added the goal, 12–22.

One of Widnes's outstanding players in the Premiership final was their scrum-half, David Hulme, who not only scored two tries but used his distributive ability to create others for his colleagues. Hulme went on to become one of the successes of the Lions' tour, playing vigorously in whatever position he was asked to fill.

The change in fortunes was amazing with Rovers now dictating and Oldham in all sorts of trouble. Another sparkling effort cracked them again as Peter Smith and Alan Banks gave winger Andy Bannister no more than a half-chance. He took it in magnificent style, cutting inside and then out to race in from forty-five yards. Quinn added another superb touchline goal to narrow the gap to 4 points and the crowd loved it.

Oldham brought on Richard Irving and Gary Warnecke for Ian Sherratt and Burke. Warnecke went to full-back, Irving on the wing with Meadows inside, and Round in the pack, changes which proved crucial. However, Rovers came again through Steadman and from deep in the Oldham '25' moved the ball crisply across to Lyman. He seemed to take the wrong option in heading for the posts and was checked, but slipped out a pass for Sykes to go over unopposed.

Quinn, cool as ever, landed the by-no-means-easy goal and Rovers were ahead 24–22.

Quinn then drove Oldham back with a solo run and seemed to clinch matters when he landed a towering forty-five yard penalty goal, his fifth in five attempts, but that was the signal for Oldham to stir themselves once more. Lyman had to make a desperate tackle at the corner to stop Irving before Rovers conceded a needless penalty to give Oldham a footing in their '25'.

It was decisive as Ford made the pass, Foy the break and Warnecke provided the link to send Meadows between the posts. McAlister's kick only just scraped over but all goals are good ones and Oldham had won amid remarkable scenes as players and fans saluted each other.

Oldham: Burke; Round, Foy, McAlister, Meadows; Walsh, Ford; Sherratt, Sanderson, Waddell, Hawkyard, Graham, Flanagan

Substitutes: Irving for Burke and Warnecke for Sherratt, both after 59 minutes.

Scorers: tries – Foy (2), Flanagan, Walsh, Meadows; goals – McAlister (4)

Featherstone Rovers: Quinn; Bannister, Sykes, Banks, Marsh; Steadman, Fox; Siddall, Bell, Harrison, Hughes, Smith, Lyman

Substitutes: Crossley for Marsh and Bastian for Siddall, both after 46 min.

Scorers: tries – Steadman (2), Bannister, Sykes; goals – Quinn (5)

Referee: M. R. Whitfield (Widnes)

Old Trafford, Manchester, 15 May

The Stones Bitter Premiership Final

St Helens 14 Widnes 38

The first-division final might have proved an anti-climax after the drama of the second division decider, but Widnes produced a performance to savour. Supremely professional and with an abundance of skill, they kept St Helens on the rack for long periods. David Hulme had an excellent game, scoring two tries to be named man-of-the-match, an award which could have gone just as easily to his team-mates Phil McKenzie, Richard Eyres or Darren Wright. Sorensen imposed himself as he wished and apart from spirited efforts by Roy Haggerty, mistake-ridden St Helens had no one to match them. Perhaps the main disappointment was that the Widnes winger, Martin Offiah, didn't score. But rarely has a man had such an effect on a match without scoring or seeing so little of the ball. St Helens were so conscious of the need to cover him that they left huge gaps elsewhere and at least three tries came because of this.

St Helens were without Phil Veivers, Chris Arkwright and Andy Platt but were given the encouragement of an early penalty-goal by Paul Loughlin. A minute later, however, their defence was horribly exposed when David Hulme's timely pass sent Kurt Sorensen charging for the line. It would have taken a lot to stop him and the only man there was Neil Holding. Holding went low, but it was like throwing a drawing pin under a tank as Sorensen went over him and the line for the first try. Duncan Platt added the goal.

The former Scottish Rugby Union centre, Alan Tait, replaced the injured Rick Thackray and went on the right wing. It looked as if he might have a testing time as Mark Bailey went through and Loughlin hit a post with a penalty attempt. Mike O'Neill made an important tackle on Paul Forber as Saints enjoyed what proved to be their one period of genuine hope, but there was always the feeling that Widnes were marking time.

After twenty-four minutes they struck hard. Phil McKenzie's break found Paul Hulme on hand and McKenzie was up for the return. He passed to Darren Wright and the whole of the stadium waited for the pass to Martin Offiah. So too did Saints and Wright used his winger as a foil to go on a curving forty-five yard run to the line for a fine try. Andy Currier added a touchline goal and it was 12–2.

From the re-start Offiah gathered and promptly kicked over the top and gave chase, accompanied by a mighty roar from the crowd. Holding had held back and cut across to make the challenge that was just enough to cause the winger to knock-on as he tried to re-gather. It made no difference. Widnes struck again when the impressive Richard Eyres brought them out of defence. The ball was moved to Offiah, who slipped out a neat pass to Eyres, who raced away before sending David Hulme over. Platt missed the easy kick but Widnes went in 16–2 at the interval.

Could Saints do a Featherstone in the second half? An early penalty goal by Loughlin raised hopes but the Widnes reply was emphatic. Currier made the break, the ever-present Eyres was in support and his fine pass again sent David Hulme to the line. Currier added the goal and at 22–4 it really was all over. St Helens produced a good move but it needed an interception by Loughlin of Barry Dowd's pass to prevent another Widnes score. The crowd rose when Offiah was given a run only to put a foot in touch.

Saints brought on Bernard Dwyer for Stuart Evans and Shaun Allen for John Fieldhouse and at last scored a try when Haggerty turned, dummied and darted over, Loughlin adding the goal. Widnes surged back through McKenzie and Offiah seemed unlucky not to get the score when Wright's inside pass bounced to him off a defender.

Widnes couldn't be kept out for long and after Eyres had gone close, Sorensen and Currier gave Tait his first try in Rugby League, to make it 26–10. A Saints flurry brought a well taken try for Barry Ledger but the Chemics shrugged off this irritation to ram home their superiority. A quick scrum heel thirty yards out enabled David Hulme to serve Wright, who went through a huge gap for the try, Currier adding a fine goal. Again St Helens had at least one eye on Offiah and they were caught again when Wright gathered a dropped pass and found the nippy McKenzie, who also took advantage of the fear of his wing colleague and showed rare pace to go in at the corner. Currier's touchline goal was a fitting finale.

It was as commanding a performance as the Premiership final has seen as Widnes joined Hull KR and Wigan in taking the trophy as champions.

St Helens: Loughlin; Ledger, Tanner, Elia, Quirk; Bailey, Holding; Burke, Groves, Evans, Forber, Fieldhouse, Haggerty

Substitutes: Dwyer for Evans after 47 minutes, Allen for Fieldhouse after 55 minutes

Scorers: tries – Haggerty, Ledger; goals – Loughlin (3)

The 1987–88 Season

Widnes: Platt; Thackray, Currier, Wright, Offiah; Dowd, David Hulme; Sorensen, McKenzie, Grima, Mike O'Neill, Paul Hulme, Eyres

Substitutes: Tait for Thackray after 9 minutes; Steve O'Neill for Grima after 58 minutes

Scorers: tries – David Hulme (2), Wright (2), Sorensen, Tait, McKenzie; goals – Platt, Currier (4)

Referee: J. Holdsworth (Kippax)

Attendance: 35,252

Martin Offiah holds high the Championship Trophy after Widnes had defeated Hunslet 66–14 in their final fixture of the 1987–88 season.

THREE

The Silk Cut Challenge Cup and the John Player Special Trophy

Paul Wilson

THE SILK CUT CHALLENGE CUP

Wigan started a trend for high drama in Challenge Cup finals in their epic 1985 encounter with Hull, a game widely received as a classic which projected the vibrancy of the sport and the personalities involved into homes throughout the world. The next two finals were perhaps less glittering occasions, but the element of drama was still present. Both Castleford, in 1986, and Halifax, in 1987, won by a single point, and in both cases the tension lasted until the final whistle.

Expectations were high, therefore, when Halifax and Wigan met on 30 April 1988. These were perhaps the two most successful sides of recent seasons, both coached by overseas strategists who had done much to introduce new tactical awareness at Thrum Hall and Central Park, and meetings between the two clubs in the league had tended to be tense, close-run affairs.

The Wembley final, however, while not exactly a disappointment, was never close enough to be interesting. Wigan started as firm favourites, and when, as the overwhelming majority of pundits had predicted, their pace in the backs began to take its toll, it became apparent all too quickly that Halifax had nothing with which to reply.

Wigan won by 32–12, becoming only the fourth team to score more than 30 points in a Wembley final. However, even this statistic conceals their superiority for they missed five of their seven kicks at goal and had two tries disallowed for borderline offside infringements. The highest score ever achieved at Wembley is 38, by Wakefield Trinity against Hull in 1960, and Halifax could not have complained if they had been on the receiving end of a new Challenge Cup final record.

One-sided finals never make great copy, and this one was all over by half-time. Wigan scored seven tries in all, some of them quite breathtaking, and put on an exhibition of powerful running rugby which made compelling viewing at times. That the game's highest honour went to the team most deserving of it there was no doubt, but those other ingredients which make finals memorable, the tension, the drama, the clash of personalities, were absent.

Halifax, although substantially the same team as the one which triumphed over St Helens the year before, were simply no match for a Wigan side stronger in almost every department than the one which set a new Wembley trend in 1985. 'Wigan,' said Maurice Lindsay, the winning chairman, 'like Wembley.

45

It's a big pitch and a big match, and that suits us down to the ground.' The Cup challenge for 1989 may be to find someone capable of giving the holders a run for their money.

Only four wins are normally needed to take a team to Wembley, but though the Challenge Cup campaign may be a short one, the experiences of the two finalists can vary widely. Such was the case in 1988, when the paths taken by Halifax and Wigan to the final were so dissimilar they were almost the opposite of each other.

The Yorkshire team managed to reach the quarter-final stage before encountering first division opposition, and their first serious examination came in the semi-final, when a titanic struggle with Hull went to a replay. Wigan, by contrast, were asked to dispose of Bradford, Leeds and Widnes, first division heavyweights all, before reaching a semi-final against Salford which probably constituted the easiest tie of their campaign.

Halifax met Heworth, the York amateurs who beat West Hull in the preliminary round, in the first round proper. Resisting strong pressure to switch the tie to Thrum Hall, the amateurs earned around £5,000 from a capacity gate at York's Wigginton Road, though their exploits on the field were not nearly so profitable. The holders thrashed them 60–4.

Kells and Leigh Miners, the other amateurs in the preliminary round, were also unable to make home advantage count, going out to Leeds and Hunslet respectively. Bramley, Huddersfield and Whitehaven were also eliminated before the first round proper, the Cumbrians having been taken to a replay by neighbouring Carlisle.

A feature of the first round draw was the high proportion of ties which paired teams from the same division. Five first-division clubs would make an early exit, while no fewer than seven second-division sides were guaranteed places in the next round. Castleford, winners of the competition in 1986, were perhaps the biggest team to fall in the first round. Over 14,000 people packed Headingley to watch the most exciting tie of the day, but despite tries by Michael Beattie and David Roockley, Leeds prevailed 22–14 thanks to a hat-trick by Paul Medley, their young international forward, and a customary try from Garry Schofield.

St Helens, after losing to Leigh in the Lancashire Cup, had reason to be wary of a return to Hilton Park, but inspired by their man-of-the-match, Phil Veivers, and two tries from Mark Elia, they came back from a 6–10 half-time deficit to win 22–12.

Swinton and Hunslet found little respite from their relegation worries in the Cup. The Mancunians, as they so often are, were drawn against neighbours Salford, and despite having the man-of-the-match in Tommy Frodsham, went down to second-half tries by Mick Worrall and Greg Austin.

Hull scarcely looked like semi-finalists at this stage, though their 27–10 victory at Hunslet was convincing enough. Paul Eastwood scored two tries, and Gary Pearce, Hull's former Welsh Rugby Union stand-off, kicked five goals and a drop-goal.

The remaining all-first-division tie was at Wigan, where Bradford were the visitors, accompanied by the BBC Grandstand cameras, interested as ever in a keenly contested trans-Pennine cup-tie. What they got, on a wet, wintry

Saturday in January, was a mud-soaked exercise in defensive sterility: a tryless, joyless match which one critic described as the best advert for Rugby Union in years. Wigan, mysteriously without Ellery Hanley, won 2–0 thanks to a long-range penalty by Joe Lydon.

Ironically, the kind of red-blooded Roses match the TV people wanted cropped up in the next round at Wigan, when the ambitious aristocrats of Leeds provided the opposition, but in the interests of a fair spread of coverage the cameras were obliged to be elsewhere.

The armchair viewer's loss was 25,180 spectators' gain. Wigan gave Leeds a 10-point start, then roared back to humble their would-be imitators 30–14. Any thoughts that Wigan, who had dropped Hanley for his alleged disruptive attitude in training in midweek, were a fading force, were quickly reappraised, though not before Medley and Schofield silenced the home crowd with tries in the opening eleven minutes.

Wigan's cause was hardly helped when Lydon left the field injured half way through the first half, but the home side steadied with tries by Andy Goodway and Brian Case, and Tony Iro's try on the stroke of half-time gave them a 16–10 interval lead. Leeds were by no means out of contention at this stage, but lost heart when Richard Russell scored for Wigan in the first minute of the second half, and could only watch helplessly as tries by Steve Hampson and Tony Iro again made the victory more emphatic.

The game which was broadcast, Warrington v. St Helens, was only marginally less spectacular, and possibly more exciting in that the lead changed hands several times before John Fieldhouse, a St Helens substitute, settled the issue with his second try three minutes from the end. Warrington, who had led for much of the game, were undone by a lapse in defensive concentration and a piece of quick thinking by Paul Groves, the St Helens hooker.

Six of the seven second-division teams which came through the first round went out at the second, the exception being Doncaster, the one team not drawn against first-division opposition. Doncaster beat Mansfield 16–8 at home, and only Featherstone and Springfield Borough put up a real fight in the David v. Goliath games. Rovers managed to score 26 points against Hull KR at Craven Park but still came away empty-handed, Mike Fletcher having scored a try and seven goals in his sides 35–26 win. Borough came even closer to a result against Salford; they were beaten 10–12 and denied a deserved replay when Mike Smith missed a penalty from in front of the posts in the last minute.

Tony Anderson scored three tries in Halifax's 30–6 win over Rochdale Hornets, and, at Keighley, Dale Shearer scored a try in his last match for Widnes to help the Cheshire side to a 16–2 victory. Hull beat Sheffield Eagles 26–6, the man-of-the-match award going to the Australian David Brooks.

Surprise and controversy, those two staples of cup rugby, arrived in the third round. The surprise was at Salford, where the home side dumped St Helens, beaten finalists the season before and strongly fancied to make a quick return, out of the competition. Perhaps Alex Murphy's side were caught with their minds already on the semi-finals, perhaps they did not imagine lowly Salford capable of beating them, but their concentration at the Willows was sadly below par. St Helens scored three tries but conceded four, Mick Worrall claiming two for the victors.

Controversy reared its head at Central Park, where Wigan, at home for a third time and with Hanley now on the transfer list at a record £225,000, won an unremittingly hard game against Widnes 10–1. Their two tries, from Hampson and Tony Iro, both came in the final quarter, when Widnes had only a drop-goal by John Myler on the board, but the Cheshire side protested vehemently that two touchdowns by Mike O'Neill and Richard Eyres, both disallowed by the Halifax referee, Jim Smith, would have altered the course of the game had they stood. In truth, Widnes appeared the superior side on the day, and it must be said that Mr Smith's decisions were hard to fathom, television replays of the touchdowns proving inconclusive. Widnes, however, felt strongly enough to ask that Mr Smith should not be allowed to officiate at their matches, though of course this could not be entertained.

There were no shocks at Hull, even though, assisted by a strong wind, Doncaster raced into a 12–6 half-time lead. With the wind at his back Pearce scored a try and four more goals as Hull swept to a 27–12 win, though the second-division team's Mark Gibson took the Silk Cut award for man-of-the-match.

A strong breeze also dominated the other quarter-final on Humberside. Hull KR had its help in the first half, but could only manage two long-range penalties from Fletcher for a 4–0 interval lead. This was never going to be enough to hold Halifax and the wind in the second half, and the holders progressed to their second semi-final in two years with two tries from Paul Dixon, and one each from Bob Grogan, Neil James and Ian Wilkinson.

Burnden Park,
Bolton,
12 March

The Challenge Cup Semi-final
Salford 4 Wigan 34

The first semi-final was overshadowed by events off the field. Peace broke out between Hanley and Wigan in time for the Great Britain captain to be included in the line-up for Bolton, and Darren Bloor, the Salford scrum-half, managed to clear himself of a one-match suspension on the eve of the game. Salford had tried to get Garry Jack back from Australia for the semi-final, but were refused permission by Balmain, his Sydney club.

In the event, the state of the pitch, rather than any of the players on or off it, proved the biggest talking-point. Bolton Wanderers had played a fourth-division soccer match against Darlington the night before, and it had not stopped raining since. Thus one of the season's vital matches was played on probably the worst surface of the winter, but though the players were indistinguishable after the first twenty minutes, Wigan's class soon made its presence felt.

Wigan had two tries on the board before the pitch began to seriously cut up, both as a result of defensive errors by Salford. Shaun Edwards was allowed far too much time to catch a hopeful chip forward by Andy Gregory, and was able to scamper to the posts through a flat-footed defence. Worse arrived for Salford in the fifteenth minute, when Steve Gibson and David Shaw collided under Hampson's kick, allowing the ball to run free close to the line. Goodway was held just short, but from a quick play-the-ball, Graeme West got Tony Iro over for the second try.

Salford conceded no further points before the interval, and began the second half in a much more determined frame of mind. Bloor slipped past Hanley and made an incisive run down the right centre's channel, releasing the ball at the right moment to give Ian Blease the try. Ken Jones missed the goal, but Salford were alive again, and for ten minutes or so the game became a struggle for supremacy.

Salford, unfancied Challenge Cup semi-finalists, never gave up against formidable opponents on a quagmire at Bolton. Their industrious scrum-half, Darren Bloor, gets the ball away from the scrum.

The try which restored Wigan's advantage and finally killed Salford's hopes was a touch lucky, not to say debatable. Hanley had the ball knocked from his grasp near the posts, and, while Salford waited for a knock-on decision, Nicky Kiss kicked ahead and touched down over the line. To Salford's horror the referee signalled a try, and was then obliged to send Steve Herbert to the sin-bin for the vehemence of his protestations.

After that there was no stopping Wigan, who scored three more tries through Kevin Iro, Edwards, and finally Hanley. The significant thing about the last from Wigan's point of view was not so much the scorer but the instigator of the move – Dean Bell, appearing as substitute for the first time after a long injury lay-off.

Salford had no real complaints after the game. Kevin Ashcroft, their coach, said: 'I thought we conceded an unlucky try at a bad time, but apart from that Wigan stuffed us.'

49

Salford: Gibson; Jones, O'Loughlin, Bentley, Shaw; Cairns, Bloor; Herbert, Moran, Disley, O'Shea, Blease, McTigue

Substitutes: Glynn for Shaw after 25 minutes, Major for McTigue at half-time

Scorer: try – Blease

Wigan: Hampson; Tony Iro, Kevin Iro, Hanley, Gill; Edwards, Gregory; Case, Kiss, Shelford, West, Potter, Goodway

Substitutes: Lucas for Shelford, Bell for West, both after 68 minutes

Scorers: tries – Edwards (2), Tony Iro, Kevin Iro, Kiss, Hanley; goals – Kevin Iro (5)

Referee: J. Holdsworth (Kippax)

Attendance: 20,783

Headingley,
Leeds,
26 March

The Challenge Cup Semi-final
Halifax 0 Hull 0

Many people thought the second semi-final would be as clear-cut as the first, with the holders taking on a team from the relegation zone, but they reckoned without an astonishing revival in Hull's fortunes, occasioned when their coach, Len Casey, walked out on the day of the Salford v. Wigan semi-final.

Hull's immediate response, once Tony Dean and Keith Hepworth had hurriedly been installed as caretaker-coaches, was to beat Halifax in their next league match. By the time of the semi-final Hull's worries about first-division

Defences held the upper hand in the two Challenge Cup semi-finals between Halifax and Hull. Here Hull's enterprising full-back, Paul Fletcher, tries to find a way past John Pendlebury, the Halifax loose forward.

survival were almost over, and Halifax were by no means certain of an easy passage to the final.

No one, however, predicted the match was going to be quite as close as it turned out. Neither side gave an inch in defence, and try-scoring chances were few and far between. On a less windy day goals might have settled the issue, but two penalty shots by Pearce were caught in the breeze, and both sides were wide with three drop-goal attempts.

Towards the end of the game, when it was apparent that just one point would suffice to book a place in the final, Hull laboriously worked a drop-goal position for Pearce under the posts, only for Terry Regan to waste the opportunity with an over-ambitious grubber kick to the line, as the stand-off waited, kicking foot poised, for the pass which never came.

It was the only blemish on Regan's otherwise admirable display, and the Australian forward's non-stop efforts in attack and defence, particularly a try-saving tackle on Martin Meredith, earned him the man-of-the-match award.

The two dressing-rooms after the game reflected how the two sides perceived the result. Hull's was happy, exuberant and full of excited chatter; Halifax's quiet, unsmiling, perhaps a little relieved. The holders blamed themselves for almost losing, while Hull, the team everyone expected to lose, talked instead of how close they came to winning.

Halifax: Eadie; Meredith, Anderson, Wilkinson, Whitfield; Grogan, Robinson; James, McCallion, Neller, Holliday, Dixon, Pendlebury

Substitutes (not used): Bell, Scott

Hull: Fletcher; Eastwood, Wilby, Gale, O'Hara; Pearce, Dick; Tomlinson, Patrick, Carroll, Regan, Brooks, Divorty

Substitutes (not used): McCaffery, Leuluai

Referee: J. McDonald (Wigan)

Attendance: 20,537

Elland Road, Leeds, 30 March	**The Challenge Cup Semi-final Replay** **Hull 3 Halifax 4**

Both teams stuck to identical line-ups from the first semi-final, Hull having gained permission to keep Scott Gale, flown from Australia especially for the Headingley match, and Brooks, also of Balmain, for the necessary three days extra.

The only thing different about the replay at Elland Road was that 5,000 more fans wanted to see it, and the kick-off had to be delayed by ten minutes to accommodate latecomers held up in traffic queues on the motorway outside the ground. When the game did get underway it was clear that little had altered from the first match. Kevin Dick crossed the line in the second minute but was recalled for a forward pass, otherwise the stalemate was very much as before. For almost half an hour the game remained scoreless, but twenty-six minutes into the game, and over 100 minutes into the semi-final, Pearce broke the deadlock with a drop-goal, to give Hull a 1–0 interval lead.

This was extended by the same player nine minutes into the second half when Halifax were penalised for crossing, and a 3–0 lead in this most miserly of contests looked as safe as a dozen points in a normal game. Hull's concentration cracked just once before the end, however, and Halifax cashed in for the single try which took them to Wembley.

Only fifteen minutes remained when Keith Neller, more in hope than expectation, slid a short kick towards Hull's left-hand corner flag, and the ball ricocheted off Brooks and hung tantalisingly over the line, just long enough for Anderson to apply fingertip pressure before Paul Fletcher booted clear. John McDonald, the referee, deserves credit for being in the right place to make a split-second decision; subsequent slow-motion replays on TV proved him absolutely correct.

After such an absorbing struggle, it was perhaps a little churlish of Chris Anderson to comment that there had been only one team in it and he had never been worried about the result. Hull were deserving of magnanimity at least. Tony Dean said: 'We were beaten by a lucky try, that's all. Halifax were going nowhere until Anderson got that touchdown.'

Hull: Fletcher; Eastwood, Wilby, Gale, O'Hara; Pearce, Dick; Tomlinson, Patrick, Carroll, Regan, Brooks, Divorty

Substitutes: McCaffery for Carroll after 67 minutes, Leuluai not used

Scorer: goal – Pearce; drop-goal – Pearce

Halifax: Eadie; Meredith, Anderson, Wilkinson, Whitfield; Grogan, Robinson; James, McCallion, Neller, Holliday, Dixon, Pendlebury

Substitutes: Bell for Eadie after 49 minutes, Scott not used

Scorer: try – Anderson

Referee: J. McDonald (Wigan)

Attendance: 25,117

Wembley
Stadium,
30 April

The Challenge Cup Final
Halifax 12 Wigan 32
The 1988 final was a sell-out almost as soon as the semi-finals were over. Halifax and Wigan are two of the best-supported clubs in the league, and each can rely on a following that is colourful and vociferous, as well as large. Halifax fans, last year's Wembley triumph fresh in their minds, were keen to repeat the experience, while Wigan's support, always impressive at a Challenge Cup final, had an appetite sharpened by two years away from the twin towers.

The behaviour of both sets of supporters was one of the big plusses of a day when events on the pitch went according to form and expectation. There was nothing wrong with the way Wigan ripped Halifax to shreds, relentlessly exposing their lack of pace and cover, but there was nothing surprising about it either.

What was surprising, especially to television viewers inured to scenes of violent conflict at soccer matches, was the way both sets of supporters happily intermingled, despite the provocation of duplicated tickets, blocked gangways and closed turnstiles. Due to some error on the part of the stadium authorities, many fans from both clubs had to watch the final from the dog-track, sitting on the floor on the pitch side of the perimeter fence.

Halifax's Graham Eadie and Bob Grogan are sent on a collision course by the speed of Shaun Edwards, who went on to create a try for Kevin Iro in the Challenge Cup final.

Such a solution would not have been risked at a soccer final, but it worked without mishap on Rugby League's day. When, after Wigan had won the Cup, some selfish fans ran on to the pitch to mob the players, they were stopped in their tracks by spontaneous chants of 'Off, Off, Off' which arose from both ends of the ground. The final itself contained barely a penalty for foul play, and the losing team was warmly applauded at the Wigan end of the ground, a gesture repaid when the winners took the Cup to the Halifax end. Sportsmanship like this is all too rare nowadays, and the behaviour of the Halifax fans was especially commendable after a final which must have broken many a Yorkshire heart.

The wide open spaces of Wembley suit some teams more than others, and Wigan, with world-class pace in almost all their back positions and an expansive, open style, were freely tipped to prosper against Halifax, notoriously short on pace, and used to playing at Thrum Hall, a ground of much less generous proportions.

Wigan had a scare in the week prior to the final when Adrian Shelford, their New Zealand prop-forward, was faced with a one-match ban for a third sin-bin offence, but he was exonerated on appeal. A much crueller fate befell Steve Hampson, the Great Britain full-back who had played a major part in getting Wigan to Wembley. Hampson broke his arm in a league game against Salford three weeks prior to the final, unbelievably missing out on his third Wembley event through injury. At least in Joe Lydon, Wigan had the ideal replacement. A Great Britain full-back himself, Lydon scarcely put a foot wrong at Wembley, and was involved in some of the most eye-catching attacking moves.

Though pressed hard by Halifax's young half-back, Steve Robinson, the Wigan captain, Shaun Edwards, makes another telling break through midfield.

Disaster struck Halifax seventeen minutes into the final, when Les Holliday twisted knee ligaments in an innocuous tackle and had to be helped from the field. This was a major blow to the Yorkshire team, who had no adequate replacement for their main kicker and ball-distributor, but though the game was still scoreless when Holliday departed, it is questionable whether he could have done much to prevent the onslaught which followed.

Gregory and Edwards had already combined sweetly to create a half-chance for Kevin Iro in the fifth minute, but the New Zealander knocked on. After twelve minutes Tony Iro won the race to touch down a Gregory kick to the right corner, only to see the try disallowed by Fred Lindop, somewhat mystifyingly on the grounds of offside.

So even before Holliday's injury, Halifax had been warned. Their fears turned into reality in the twenty-fourth minute, when Gregory put Edwards away on a damaging break through the middle, and though the young Wigan captain was pulled down a yard short, a recent hamstring injury having taken the edge off his pace, Kevin Iro backed up quickly to muscle over from the play-the-ball. Two minutes later Hanley went on a surging run, which would have brought a try but for a misunderstanding between the Iros, and two minutes after that Wigan registered their second try when Gregory and Bell sent Henderson Gill striding to the left corner.

Halifax were already starting to look shell-shocked, but worse was to come. Tony Iro gathered from the restart and broke straight through some dispirited Halifax tackling to present his brother with his second try. In a little over six minutes Wigan had struck three times and the final was all over bar the shouting. The only glimmer of hope for Halifax was that Wigan kept missing the goals. Even when Lydon crossed by the posts on the stroke of half-time, after splendid work by Edwards, Gregory, the third kicker used by Wigan, managed to slap his kick against an upright.

Halifax's Paul Dixon cannot stop the powerful run of Wigan's Ellery Hanley. Two of the stalwarts of a powerful Wigan pack, Adrian Shelford and Ian Potter, are in support.

It is difficult to imagine a more forlorn place than the Halifax dressing-room at half-time. What, if anything, Chris Anderson had to say about the 16–0 deficit is not recorded, but he must have been as acutely aware as his players that Wembley is a very public place to endure another forty minutes of torment.

It took Wigan six minutes to extend their lead, but the pass with which Gregory gave Tony Iro an easy touchdown on the right was worth a longer wait. Aware that players were bumping into themselves in the middle, Gregory floated a long ball out to the right, a tantalising pass which Colin Whitfield thought he could reach then realised he couldn't. With Whitfield stranded on the ground, Iro accepted the pass without breaking his stride, and strolled to the line unchallenged. Gregory, a clear winner of the Lance Todd Trophy, had a hand in most of the Wigan tries, but never was his positional awareness better demonstrated.

Halifax wearily restarted the game, only to find themselves back under their posts in a matter of seconds. Gregory had fielded the kick-off and fed Lydon, who cut an elegant swathe through the right hand side of the Halifax defence and took the ball right back into the danger area before unloading to Hanley, who kept out of reach of the cover in a sideways run to the posts. Gregory kicked the first Wigan goal from their sixth try, and with half an hour of the game left, the final was beginning to look like a case for the League Against Cruel Sports.

Wigan's spate dried up as suddenly as it had started, however, and it was Halifax, showing commendable heart, who scored the next try, when Ian Wilkinson put Tony Anderson over in the right corner. To ironic cheers from both ends of the ground, Whitfield added the goal from the touchline.

Wigan were not quite finished. Another break involving Gregory and Edwards was continued by Hanley and finished with a try by Bell, Lydon adding the goal this time. A minute later Gregory was unlucky for a second time when he kicked through for Tony Iro to touch down, but the score was disallowed for another borderline offside.

Halifax had the last say, when Neil James showed a nimble change of direction for a prop-forward to score by the posts, but all the glory in the end belonged to Wigan. 'No one in the world would have beaten you out there today,' Graham Lowe told his players after the lap of honour. Chris Anderson was unable to disagree. 'Wigan were much too strong and fast for us,' he said.

Halifax: Eadie; Meredith, Anderson, Wilkinson, Whitfield; Grogan, Robinson; James, McCallion, Neller, Holliday, Dixon, Pendlebury

Substitutes: Scott for Holliday after 17 minutes, Fairbank for Robinson after 47 minutes

Scorers: tries – Anderson, James; goals – Whitfield (2)

Wigan: Lydon; Tony Iro, Kevin Iro, Bell, Gill; Edwards, Gregory; Case, Kiss, Shelford, Goodway, Potter, Hanley

Substitutes: Byrne for Edwards after 75 minutes, Wane for Potter after 76 minutes

Scorers: tries – Kevin Iro (2), Gill, Lydon, Tony Iro, Hanley, Bell; goals – Gregory, Lydon.

Referee: G. F. Lindop (Wakefield)

Attendance: 94,273

Receipts: £1,102,247

When Alex Murphy returned to St Helens as coach in November 1985 he styled himself The Messiah. The twenty-six months it took him to deliver the Knowsley Road faithful their promised success was perhaps a longer wait than first envisaged, though in the context of the club's record in the John Player Special Trophy it was quick work indeed.

Following his side's victory over Leeds by a single point in an absorbing final at Wigan, Murphy was able to claim he had achieved something none of his coaching predecessors had managed. The John Player Special Trophy was the one prize which had always eluded St Helens who, after no fewer than five failures at the semi-final stage, had never previously contested a final.

Leeds, by contrast, were appearing in their fourth final, and trying to win the trophy for a record-equalling third time. Their thoughtfully assembled team of expensive British players and top-quality Australians had disposed of Wigan, the favourites, in a memorable semi-final at Bolton, after which the bookmakers were quick to shorten the odds on Maurice Bamford's side for the final.

Murphy, a gambling man himself, suggested a week before the final that it was ridiculous to have such clear favourites in a two-horse race, but his comments seemed to be founded more on optimism than observation. St Helens had not looked convincing in beating Oldham of the second division in the semi-final, and their indifferent season so far had been overshadowed by events off the pitch.

The eleventh-hour collapse of negotiations with David Bishop, a Welsh international Rugby Union scrum-half, had attracted a good deal of un-favourable publicity, and St Helens came out of their wrangle with Wigan over Adrian Shelford with even less dignity. A High Court judge, no less, awarded the New Zealand Test forward to the Central Park club, and all costs against St Helens.

The judge's decision came in mid-December, severely curtailing festive cheer at Knowsley Road, but a timely boost to sagging morale came from where it was least expected – Central Park. St Helens staged a remarkable fightback to recover from a 6–22 half-time deficit to win the Boxing Day derby at Wigan 32–22 and, when they returned to face Leeds on the same ground two weeks later, they found they had the edge in the crucial department of self-belief.

Phil Veivers, Saints' Australian full-back, identified the earlier Central Park victory as the turning-point of the season: 'After coming back like that against Wigan, we were ready for anything.'

After the final defeat of Leeds, Murphy talked of game-plans and strategies, but was not too proud to admit relief: 'After the season we've had, we needed that,' he said.

St Helens had been involved in the tie of the first round, when they needed all their resourcefulness to overcome a strong challenge from Widnes at Knowsley Road, though interest in the town had been awakened earlier, due to the presence of local amateurs Thatto Heath in the preliminary round.

Coached by Frank Barrow, a Saints player in the 1960s, Thatto Heath were in the competition as holders of the BNFL National Cup, and were rewarded with a draw few professional teams would have relished, away to Featherstone Rovers.

'Post Office Road has just become our Wembley,' commented a Heath official at the draw. Wembley or not, the amateurs lost 16–34 after a brave fight, though some consolation for Barrow came the same weekend when Swinton, to whom he had just been appointed assistant coach, won 32–5 against Heworth of York, the other amateur team in the preliminary round. Featherstone and Swinton were joined in the first round proper by Oldham and York, convincing winners in their ties against Fulham and Bramley respectively.

The first round was full of potentially interesting ties between first and second division clubs, and yielded several surprisingly close scores and two genuine upsets. These came at Batley, where first division Hunslet went out 16–18, and at Oldham, where Eric Fitzsimons's promising new side completely outplayed Bradford Northern, the Yorkshire Cup holders, to win 22–6.

Elsewhere, Warrington and Leeds were getting bogged down in Cumbrian mud. Tony Barrow's side left it late before winning 22–16 at Carlisle, and at Whitehaven, Lee Crooks, Garry Schofield and the other expensive Headingley acquisitions had an even bigger scare, needing a hotly disputed penalty try to help them to a lucky 18–14 victory.

In the two all-first-division ties, a Mick McTigue try eventually brought Salford an 18–12 win over Swinton in a bad-tempered Station Road derby, and though Widnes scored two tries to the home side's one, Martin Offiah's last minute touchdown at St Helens came too late to prevent a 10–12 defeat.

Home teams prospered in seven of the eight second-round games, the exception being at Batley, where Oldham's 44–0 success suggested the Gallant Youths had had enough of giant-killing for one season. St Helens also scored 40 points to no reply against Mansfield; Leeds looked much more solid in disposing of Halifax at Headingley, and Wigan came to life with a vibrant 26–16 victory over Castleford.

The holders had looked sluggish in beating Sheffield Eagles in the first round, Joe Lydon's infamous head-butt epitomising an off-colour day, but inspired by Kevin Iro, their young New Zealand centre, Wigan scored four stylish tries to take them through.

Hull Kingston Rovers were unlucky to go out in a tense struggle at Warrington, where Gordon Smith, of the losing side, was named man of the match, and, before another disappointing crowd at Springfield Park, little-fancied Springfield Borough beat Wakefield Trinity 14–8 to join their illustrious neighbours in the draw for the third round.

Borough wanted Wigan at home, but had to be content with possibly the next best thing, Leeds. Once again, in muddy conditions, the first-division side did not have things all their own way, but two tries by David Creasser and a memorable solo score by Steve 'Slippery' Morris helped Leeds to a 22–12 win.

Wigan needed a last-minute try by Shaun Edwards, his second of the game, to see off a spirited Salford side at the Willows, and St Helens had to come from behind to beat Hull 20–16 at Knowsley Road, but the shock of the round came at Wilderspool, where Oldham put out Warrington, last year's beaten finalists.

Anyone studying the progress of the two teams in the earlier rounds might have predicted just such a result, but the comprehensiveness of the second-division side's win still took most people by surprise. Oldham were particularly impressive in the forwards, where they had outstanding servants in Hugh Waddell and Neil Clawson, and their teamwork and organisation in defence was of the highest order.

Tries in either half by Terry Flanagan and Paul Round, with three goals from Peter Walsh, brought Oldham a fully deserved 14–10 victory, Warrington's points coming from a Paul Cullen try and three John Woods' goals. 'We didn't underestimate them,' said a bemused Tony Barrow after the match. 'We just didn't play as well as they did.'

The first semi-final brought together Wigan and Leeds, to the disappointment of those who thought the meeting of the most successful side of recent seasons and their most ambitious challengers would have made the ideal final.

Leeds had grown in stature steadily throughout the season as more calibre players were added to the Headingley mix, and by the time of the semi-final, played on a crisp December afternoon at Burnden Park, they were a more settled side than Wigan, who had lost Dean Bell and Nicky Kiss through injury, and whose pack included two youngsters, Ian Lucas and Ian Gildart, in place of the vastly more experienced Ian Potter and Graeme West. The stage was set for a classic confrontation, and the game did not disappoint.

Leeds suffered two early setbacks, the loss of Crooks with a dislocated shoulder in the opening minutes, and the defensive lapse on the left wing which let in Steve Hampson for the opening try; but by half-time, with substitute forward Kevin Rayne playing one of the most effective games of his long career, and Paul Medley on the scoresheet after a splendid frontal assault on the Wigan defence, the scores were level at 6–6.

The opening of the second half was predictably tense, so much so that Ray Ashton deemed a drop-goal a worthwhile investment, but it was always likely that something special would be needed to settle the tie. Wigan went close with a couple of flashing handling movements, but it was Schofield at the other end who provided the decisive score, extending the Leeds lead with a try fit to win any semi-final. The costliest player among two costly sides surged into a gap in front of the posts before leaving Hampson floundering with a thundering change of direction.

Colin Maskill's goal left Wigan needing to score twice, but the holders had nothing in reserve, and Maskill added a try and a third goal to complete a decisive 19–6 win.

The second semi-final could not help but suffer by comparison after the excitement of Bolton, and there was an air of anti-climax as St Helens competently but unimaginatively accounted for Oldham 18–8 at Central Park.

Oldham's reserves of concentration and stamina appeared to have been exhausted at Warrington, though St Helens did not have the semi-final all their own way. The second-division team did most of the pressing in the first quarter, only to see St Helens score first as a result of their first serious attack, Andy Platt's try after twenty minutes being goaled by Paul Loughlin.

Saints, by Murphy's own admission, then 'went to sleep' for half an hour, allowing Oldham to take the lead through tries by Bryan McCarthy and Garry Warnecke, both Australians, either side of the interval. Losing the lead only stung St Helens into action, however, and within seven minutes they had regained the advantage with a try by Roy Haggerty and another Loughlin goal. This time Oldham could not come back, and Shane Cooper's try four minutes from time, goaled, like the others, by Loughlin, put St Helens in their first-ever John Player final.

Murphy highlighted his team's tackling afterwards. 'We have been able to come from behind in almost every round,' he said. 'We no longer go to pieces when people score against us. We can limit the damage, and take our chances at the other end.'

Central Park,
Wigan,
9 January

The John Player Special Trophy Final
Leeds 14 St Helens 15

St Helens surprised everyone in the final, not just by beating the favourites, but by displaying a hitherto unsuspected appetite for tackling.

Knowsley Road teams have always been capable of fluent attacking football and brilliant tries as a result of off-the-cuff invention, though they have frequently let down their followers by adopting a similarly cavalier attitude to the more mundane but equally important duties involved in defence.

When Roy Powell brushed aside two tacklers to set up the first Leeds try for Creasser after thirteen minutes, many St Helens supporters must have feared the worst. Creasser added the goal to give Leeds a 6-point lead, but St Helens were able to answer back quickly with first a penalty, then a try and a goal from Loughlin, whose 14-point contribution to his side's 15-point total was to earn him the man-of-the-match award.

Leeds were unhappy about the try, which they claimed followed a St Helens knock-on, but there seemed no reason to panic. Creasser levelled the scores at 8–8 with a penalty on the half-hour, then Leeds took advantage of a typical piece of St Helens generosity to gain the lead for a second time. Peter Souto, heavily tackled by Medley, lost the ball inside his own '25', and it was transferred in an instant to the unguarded left wing, where Peter Jackson touched down before the challenge arrived from Veivers, his former Brisbane Souths team-mate. Creasser improved the score with a towering kick from the touchline, but though Leeds could not have known it at the time, a more significant kick was Neil Holding's drop-goal, two minutes before the interval, which reduced the St Helens arrears to 14–9.

Murphy's half-time message was simple: 'Score a quick try!' Loughlin was able to oblige within a minute of the restart, combining well with Platt and Veivers on the right wing before stepping round the stricken Marty Gurr and running unchallenged to the posts. His goal, or perhaps more precisely Holding's, put St Helens one point in front, and though few imagined the score would stay that way, no one, including Leeds, had come prepared for a Saints stonewall action.

To the mounting disbelief of both sets of supporters, the rest of the second half was played out on or around the St Helens 25-yard line, as wave after wave of Leeds attacks were repulsed by an increasingly confident defence. St Helens

Alex Murphy, the St Helens coach, during the
John Player Trophy final. In a match of
swaying fortunes, St Helens beat Leeds by the
narrowest of margins to win the Trophy for
the first time.

Leeds disappointed their supporters in the John Player final against St Helens, though no player tried harder than Roy Powell, whose strong run set up Leeds's first try.

could not even kick their way out of trouble – punts downfield from Veivers and Loughlin were returned almost instantly – but, despite an embarrassment of possession, Leeds displayed a certain lack of imagination and guile in their often predictable assaults on the thin red-and-white line.

What was even more culpable was their disdain for the drop-goal option, which could have earned a replay, or at least brought St Helens out of their shell. Only seven minutes were left when a somewhat desperate Schofield took a shy at goal, and when his well struck kick slapped against an upright Leeds must have sensed it was not to be their day. St Helens made sure Leeds were not allowed another chance, and actually ended the game on their opponents' line, but Paul Forber's last-minute touchdown was disallowed by Fred Lindop, the referee.

Leeds were disappointed afterwards, but had no grounds for complaint. 'We had enough chances,' said Bamford. 'St Helens deserved their win.'

Leeds: Gurr; Morris, Schofield, Jackson, Basnett; Creasser, Ashton; Tunks, Maskill, Rayne, Powell, Medley, Heron

Substitutes: Gibson for Basnett and Fairbank for Rayne, both after 70 minutes

Scorers: tries – Creasser, Jackson; goals – Creasser (3)

St Helens: Veivers; Tanner, Loughlin, Elia, Quirk; Cooper, Holding; Burke, Groves, Souto, Forber, Haggerty, Platt

Substitutes: Evans for Souto after 64 minutes, Large not used

Scorers: tries – Loughlin (2); goals – Loughlin (3); drop-goal – Holding

Referee: G. F. Lindop (Wakefield)

Attendance: 16,669

Steve Hampson was chaired by his team-mates after Wigan's Challenge Cup final victory. Hampson won the sympathy of all in the game after a broken arm once again ruled him out of a Wembley final.

FOUR

The British Coal Nines Tournament

Ray French

The announcement of the first-ever British Coal nine-a-side tournament, to be held at Central Park, Wigan on the night of 28 October 1987, was greeted in Rugby League circles with a considerable degree of surprise and, later, expectancy. Traditionalists, who saw any watering down of the thirteen-a-side game as a bastardisation of the code, frowned; lovers of the usual seven-a-side version were intrigued by the need to include two extra forwards; while coaches and players reflected on the tactics that should be used.

Would there be the usual free-flowing back play of the customary seven-a-side tournament? Would the two extra forwards hinder all attempts at providing a spectacle of Rugby League skills? Would those two extra players prove too effective in the tackle to allow sides in matches of seven minutes each way to score the tries which the fans had come to see? But whatever the questions, the prospect of seeing the top six teams from the previous season's Stones Bitter Championship and the two touring teams, Papua New Guinea and Auckland, displaying their skills tempted a good crowd of 6,859 spectators to Central Park on a cold dry evening and enabled many millions more to enjoy the spectacle in their homes thanks to BBC TV's Sportsnight programme.

Bob Ashby, the Rugby League's chairman, was proved right when he declared that the nine-a-side format was designed 'to reflect the traditional skills of Rugby League'. With five players forming a pack and all matches being played under the six-tackle rule there was still a need for solid scrummaging, strong running, and hard tackling from the forwards while the backs, given more room in which to work, could indulge in a variety of handling and running skills. The matches thus proved to be a mini version of the thirteen-a-side game and not, as with seven-a-side, almost a completely different game.

Most coaches and players approached the tournament with a completely open mind and many intended to use the opening round to help them formulate tactics but it was obvious that many had, before the kick-off, already thought carefully about the requirements for success. The Castleford coach, Dave Sampson, had realised the necessity of fielding young fit players to last out the hectic pace of the matches and included many Colts players in his squad, such as Kenny Hill, Dean Sampson, and Ian Hardisty, who all did well. The Wigan coach, Graham Lowe, had worked on a variety of set ploys and defensive strategies and the disciplined approach of his side was a major factor in his team's appearance in the final. Fielding a traditional pack of five forwards, the St Helens coach Alex Murphy was honest enough to admit that, 'For next season's competition I would play nine backs in my side, using two big centres as second rowers, such is the pace of nine-a-side rugby'. Whatever

Ellery Hanley, the Great Britain captain, takes the ball before his marvellous first-half try against the Australians in the first Test in Sydney.

Kevin Ward crashes through the Australian defence in the first Test. Peter Sterling is on the left of the picture, Paul Vautin on the right.

below Paul Vautin, the Australian second-rower, is held by Mike Gregory and Andy Platt, with Ellery Hanley in attendance, during the first Test.

Andy Gregory evades the attempted tackle of
Martin Bella, making his international debut,
in the third Test in Sydney.

below Wayne Pearce is unable to escape Roy
Powell's tackle while his second-row partner
Mike Gregory stands by in support in the third
Test.

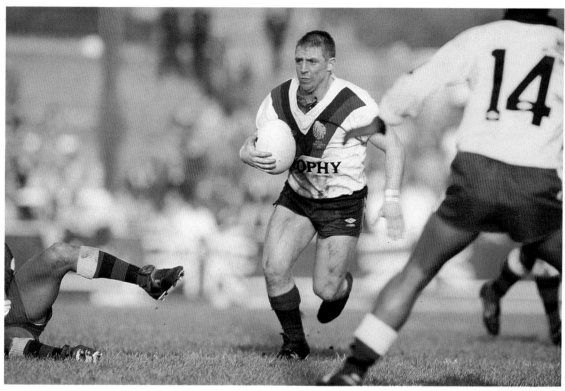

Andy Gregory, the Great Britain scrum-half, makes a break during the Test against Papua New Guinea at Wigan and is confronted by the Papuan substitute, Mathias Kitimun.

below Roy Powell is tackled by the French number 8, Marc Tissèyre, during the Avignon Test against France.

Shane Horo, playing for Auckland in their tour match against Leeds, is halted by a determined Leeds tackle.

below Yorkshire celebrate their defeat of Lancashire by 16–10 in the Rodstock War of the Roses match. Yorkshire's coach, Peter Fox, is in the centre.

Neil James of Halifax, supported by Seamus McCallion, is halted by the tackle of the Wigan centre, Dean Bell, in the Challenge Cup final.

below David Hulme, the Widnes scrum-half, gets his pass away, despite the attentions of St Helens defenders, during the Premiership final.

Kurt Sorensen, the Widnes captain, on his way to a barnstorming try in the Premiership final, outpacing the St Helens full-back, Paul Loughlin, and their winger Les Quirk.

below Darren Wright, of Widnes, tries to hand-off the St Helens full-back, Paul Loughlin, in the Premiership final.

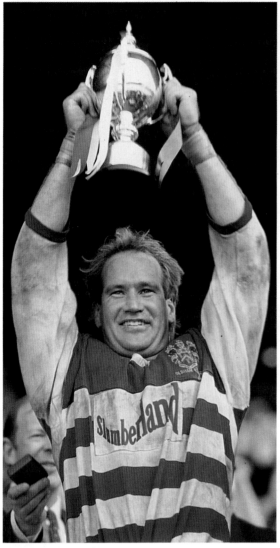

Mal Graham, Oldham's captain, holds high the
second division Premiership Trophy after their
splendid win against Featherstone Rovers.

Kurt Sorensen, the Widnes captain, holds up
the Premiership Trophy after defeating St
Helens 38–14 in the final at Old Trafford.

The Castleford Winger, David Plange, makes a determined run in the British Coal Nines final against Wigan, whose defence remained unbreached, however.

the approach or views of the coaches it was an unusually quiet crowd who watched the tactics of the first three matches unfold.

As teams grappled to come to terms with the tactical complexities the interest of the large Wigan contingent in the crowd was first aroused by the sight of their new Kiwi signing, 19-year-old Kevin Iro, appearing in the colours of Auckland. A well taken try by the strong running Iro, in his side's 8–0 defeat of a sluggish Halifax side, set them in good mood for the final match of the opening round between their cherry-and-white favourites and the exciting newcomers from Papua New Guinea. Applauded off the field at Central Park at the end of their first-ever Test match appearance in Great Britain on the previous Saturday, they roused the fans even more, especially the Wigan faithful, when they sped into a 4–0 lead within a minute of the start of play.

Though slight in stature it was expected that, in the nine-a-side variety, the Kumuls handling and running abilities would far outweigh the physical problems they had encountered on the tour of Great Britain when playing under normal thirteen-a-side rules. They did not disappoint and, after some breathtaking handling, even the Wigan supporters had to cheer the try scored by Clement Mou which gave them their shock lead. This try signalled the arrival of the British Coal Nines as a competitive tournament, and the crowd, earlier

65

quietly appreciative, were now aroused in a display of passionate interest. Sadly for the Kumuls the mini-version of Rugby League did require big strong forwards and Wigan, roared on by their enthusiastic supporters, used their heavier pack-men, Graeme West and Andy Goodway, to good effect, finally winning the match by 12–4. The match was notable for a fine performance by the Wigan youngster Richard Russell who, though only kicking a goal in this first-round match, displayed the appetite for the competition which was eventually to reward him with the British Coal man-of-the-series award.

In the semi-finals Auckland, who had been confidently tipped beforehand to do well, struggled against the youthful Castleford side. The Kiwis rarely mastered the delicate balance needed of strong forward driving and carefree back running and, as a result, indulged in far too many one-man plunges down the middle. Such tactics proved futile against the strong tackling of the Castleford pack. Kevin Iro again was their lone scorer with a try and a conversion. In contrast Castleford, sensibly using an experienced wing, Gary Hyde, in their second row, had far too much pace for the Auckland team and moved the ball out wide at every opportunity. Gary Hyde, surprising the Auckland defenders with his extra yard of pace, crossed for two tries and Roy Southernwood and the wing, David Plange, added two more. Giles Boothroyd

Wigan's nine – a combination of youth and experience – celebrate their victory in the inaugural British Coal Nines final.

and Bob Beardmore converted two tries to win the match by the most convincing score of the night, 20–6.

Any St Helens v. Wigan match is guaranteed to raise the temperature but, despite the closeness of the score at half time, 4–0 in Wigan's favour, the enthusiasm of the large band of Saints supporters was dampened by the strong forceful play of the Wigan forwards who absorbed all the St Helens attacks with a solid defensive wall. And the quick thinking of the youngsters Ged Byrne and Richard Russell resulted in tries to add to that of skipper Graeme West. Russell increased his night's points tally to 10 with two well taken conversions. A 16–0 victory for Wigan put their fans in hopeful mood for the final. And they were not to be disappointed.

Surprisingly the final, extended to nine minutes each way, did not produce the harvest of points many expected, the only scores being in the second half after an earlier dour nine minutes. The first half proved to be a struggle between both packs of forwards with defences so tight that rarely a break was made by any player on either side. For Castleford, the young forward, Ken Hill, worked overtime, stemming any attacks with fine cover tackles, yet still finding the energy to bring the ball away from deep inside his own half. But always there was the threat of a breakaway by one of the highly priced Wigan stars. Richard Russell, revelling in the extra space afforded for back play, put Wigan ahead with a try and a conversion, leaving Ellery Hanley to display his talents by scoring a try to make the winning margin 10–0.

Wigan proved worthy winners of the inaugural competition, fielding the right blend of player with both the size and speed of such as Ellery Hanley, Richard Russell, Andy Goodway, and David Marshall. With a £25,000 sponsorship, generously provided by British Coal, including the handsome sum of £6,000 for the winners, the experiment had proved a successful venture for all eight teams involved. The Rugby League code's image had been enhanced, for over a hundred minutes of fast exciting rugby had been set before the fans on the terraces and before millions on television. It had proved to be an experiment well worth continuing.

at Central Park, Wigan, Wednesday, 28 October 1987

Castleford	*Hull KR*	*Warrington*	*St Helens*
David Roockley	Steve Smith	Mark Forster	Phil Veivers
David Plange	Tony Sullivan	Mike Bacon	Kevin McCormack
Michael Beattie	Peter Mortimer	Ron Duane	Les Quirk
Giles Boothroyd	John Lydiat	Joe Ropati	Roy Haggerty
Gary Hyde	Mike Smith	Damion Gregory	Barry Ledger
Roy Southernwood	George Fairbairn	Martin Crompton	Mark Bailey
Bob Beardmore	Wayne Parker	Phil Capewell	David Tanner
Dean Sampson	Ross Taylor	Darren Harris	Paul Forber
Kenny Hill	Chris Rudd	John Thursfield	Paul Groves
John Fifita	Zook Ema	Mark Knight	Tony Burke
Ian Hardisty	Glenn Ryan	Stephen Molloy	Andy Platt

Halifax	*Auckland*	*Papua New Guinea*	*Wigan*
Mick Taylor	John Ropati	Mat Kitimun	Dave Marshall
Eddie Riddlesden	Warren Mann	James Kapia	Ged Byrne
Robert Grogan	Kevin Iro	Michael Matmillo	David Stephenson
Brian Juliffe	Shane Cooper	Ngala Lapan	Richard Russell
Simon Longstaff	Mike Patton	Elias Kamiak	Martin Dermott
Dean Hanson	Paddy Tuimavave	Bob Ako	Andrew Goodway
Scott Wilson	Rene Nordmeyer	Clement Mou	Ellery Hanley
Neil James	Peter Ropati	Roy Heni	Graeme West
Graham Eadie	Sam Panapa	Dairi Kovae	Ian Lucas
Ian Wilkinson	Shane Horo	Kepi Saea	Ian Gildart
Keith Neller	Tea Ropati	Arnold Krewanty	Denis Betts

Round 1	Castleford	8	(tries – Beattie, Plange)
	v		
	Hull KR	6	(try – Steve Smith; goal – Fairbairn)
	Halifax	0	
	v		
	Auckland	8	(tries – Iro, Panapa)
	Warrington	10	(tries – Duane, Knight; goal – Crompton)
	v		
	St Helens	14	(tries – Veivers, Quirk, Ledger; goal – Forber)
	Papua New Guinea	4	(try – Mou)
	v		
	Wigan	12	(tries – Marshall, Goodway; goals – Stephenson, Russell)
Semi-finals	Castleford	20	(tries – Hyde (2), Southernwood, Plange; goals – Beardmore, Boothroyd)
	v		
	Auckland	6	(try – Iro; goal – Iro)
	St Helens	0	
	v		
	Wigan	16	(tries – West, Byrne, Russell; goal – Russell)
Final	Castleford	0	
	v		
	Wigan	10	(tries – Russell, Hanley; goal – Russell)

The British Coal man-of-the-series: Richard Russell (Wigan)

Referees: G. F. Lindop (Wakefield), J. Holdsworth (Kippax)

Attendance: 6,859

FIVE

The Grünhalle Lager Lancashire Cup and the John Smith's Yorkshire Cup

Mike Rylance

THE GRÜNHALLE LAGER LANCASHIRE CUP

The Lancashire Cup competition, reflecting perhaps the hospitable nature of Lancashire people, has long been open to clubs from outside the county boundaries. In 1987, however, the teams from farthest afield found once again that the hospitality does not extend to the field of play. Geographically speaking, the competition shrank, after the first round, by several hundred miles as Fulham and Carlisle in particular failed to penetrate the closed ranks of the more established teams.

Though there were, thankfully, no scores as huge as Carlisle's 0–112 defeat at this stage in the previous year, there were several high-scoring matches, typical of the early season, when attitudes towards defence have not yet hardened. In addition to Fulham's 4–58 defeat by Salford, in which Steve Gibson, the lesser-known of Salford's two Australian full-backs, played a significant part, there were convincing defeats for Barrow, Runcorn and, more surprisingly, Oldham. Barrow surrendered to Wigan's speed and power and lost 2–36, though Runcorn put up a fight, almost literally, against neighbours Widnes before losing 6–40 in a match in which three players were sent off and two others sin-binned. In another rough match, newly relegated Oldham could prove nothing to Warrington, who were inspired by the man-of-the-match, John Woods, to run up 42 points to 8. At Swinton, 58 points were scored; Rochdale led at half-time, but suffered the second-half loss of their player-coach Eric Hughes, an old hand at this competition, and went down 20–38.

The closest match of the first round was disputed outside the county. Springfield Borough, who had beaten a retreat from Blackpool to regather at Wigan, appeared for the first time in this guise. They could not assert their new identity at Workington and lost 10–12. In an entirely non-Lancashire affair, Carlisle fell to the equally Cumbrian but, in Rugby League terms, less exotic Whitehaven, who went through 28–12.

Cup competitions wouldn't be the same without at least one shock result, which was provided, not for the only time in the season, by St Helens. With both coaches having been in charge at one time or another of the other's club, it was the former St Helens player and coach, Billy Benyon, who laughed longest as Leigh, 10 points down in the last quarter, pulled back to win 27–21. But that was as far as Leigh got. In the second round they lost to Swinton, whom they had never before beaten in this competition. Swinton, well led by Les Holliday, ran up 16 points in the first quarter of an hour and emerged as winners by

22–14. The eventual finalists also settled the outcome of their second-round matches early on. Wigan outclassed Salford to lead 28–2 in the first half and added 14 more points in the second half without reply. Style-conscious Ellery Hanley, with his penchant for changing to a numberless jersey at half-time, was far from anonymous and scored two tries. Conspicuous also was the powerful Andy Goodway, playing at prop. This, allied to the zip of Andy Gregory and Shaun Edwards, was a cut above what Salford could offer. Warrington similarly overpowered Workington, amassing 50 points against 10. The final match of the round, played the following day, was also the keenest. Widnes were made to struggle by a determined Whitehaven, who were level at the interval before a second Martin Offiah try decided the issue and Widnes came through by 20–14.

Warrington's progress through the semi-final stage was not unduly troubled by Swinton, who were virtually out of the competition by half-time, when the score was 26–0. The final score of 44–6 gave Warrington a points total of 136 for the three rounds, with Woods contributing fifty of them. The other semi-final, between Widnes and Wigan, was much more closely contested. In a tense game, Wigan took the lead through an Edwards try which resulted from a storming run by Henderson Gill. The immensely influential Kurt Sorensen countered for Widnes with a superb break and pass to Offiah, whose pace did the rest. A Goodway try from a penalty move then took Wigan to a 12–6 interval lead.

In the second half, Widnes applied relentless pressure but failed to crack Wigan's stern defence. In a game of such high standards it was ironically a mis-timed drop-goal attempt that did duty as a grubber kick which settled the issue in Wigan's favour. David Stephenson followed up his own kick and fell on the ball over the line for Wigan's third try and a 20–12 victory which took them to meet Warrington in a reprise of the 1985 final.

The Lancashire Cup Final

Knowsley Road, St Helens, 11 October

Wigan 28 Warrington 16

It was Wigan's fourth consecutive Lancashire Cup final and possibly the one they were least looking forward to. Only four days had elapsed since their brilliant victory over Manly in the unofficial world club challenge match – surely one of the most intense club matches ever played in Britain. In contrast the Lancashire Cup seemed more than usually parochial. More than that, it was the culmination of a particularly heavy programme. 'The Manly game took more out of us than people realised,' said the Wigan coach, Graham Lowe, 'because of all the international prestige attached to it. We were physically and mentally drained. In fact I was more worried about the mental pressure than anything else.'

Warrington, without attracting quite so much of the glory or the headlines as their opponents, were heading the first division. Though they had suffered from injuries to several key players, they were spurred not only by the usual local rivalry but also by the memory of the 1985 defeat.

Another 20,000 crowd saw Warrington make the first thrusts, with a try materialising after twelve minutes. Brian Johnson's diagonal run in the Wigan '25' started a move for Mark Forster to score from Mike Gregory's pass. With a

0–6 deficit, Wigan were finding life hard but Shaun Edwards's break to send Ellery Hanley on a run gave promise of things to come. The promise was fulfilled when, following a scrum near the Warrington line, Henderson Gill, with an abrupt change of direction, crossed for an unconverted try.

Despite the two tries, both defences were uncompromising. Warrington especially, whose forwards were playing like a set of very athletic bears, well led by Kevin Tamati, looked to be giving their opponents something of a mauling. There were times when Wigan appeared disorganised in the face of Warrington's forward strength and things looked bad for them when they went further behind as John Woods converted Mike Gregory's try to make it 12–4.

Then Andy Gregory, perhaps fearing a fourth loser's medal, took a hand. His pass was taken by Andy Goodway on the burst; Goodway passed on to Hanley, who crossed the line with Edwards directing his captain to go between the posts. David Stephenson converted easily, then left the field to be replaced by Dean Bell, returning from injury. Shortly after, the goal-kicking duties fell to Joe Lydon, who kicked a huge penalty goal, and then another to give Wigan a half-time lead.

A familiar sight: a Wigan captain holding the Lancashire Cup. Ellery Hanley led his team to their third successive win and their nineteenth overall in this competition.

Wigan's commitment to an expansive style of play had begun to pay off. It contrasted with Warrington's determination to play to their forwards and half-backs, where the ex-Wigan player, Keith Holden, served his stand-off partner, John Woods, particularly well.

The styles, if not the scoring, followed a similar pattern in the second half. Wigan's passing was at times over-ambitious but made an exciting spectacle, enhanced by Steve Hampson's runs out of defence. Wigan also made use of a variety of kicks, which, if fielded or cleared dead by Drummond or Carbert, at least gave the Warrington wingers something to do.

After another Lydon penalty goal, the Warrington half-backs instigated a telling move. Woods, more cultured than a string of pearls, made one of his many breaks which led to Forster's second try. The scores were even again and Wigan were looking decidedly harassed.

It was the irrepressible Edwards who seized back the initiative for Wigan. His smart break from a set play put Hanley in for his second try and with ten minutes left it was now Warrington who were short of time and ideas. Wigan meanwhile were getting their third or fourth wind. Bell suddenly burst on to Gregory's pass and, when he was half-stopped, passed on to substitute Graeme West, who went over the line in triumph. At 28–16 the game was out of Warrington's reach, but Wigan forgot their tiredness and until the end remained inventive and enthusiastic in their support play. It was an example of the 'sheer guts' to which Graham Lowe paid tribute as his team retained their unique association with this old trophy.

Warrington: Johnson; Drummond, Forster, Peters, Carbert; Woods, Holden; Tamati, Webb, Humphries, Sanderson, Roberts, Mike Gregory

Substitutes: Harmon for Webb after 7 minutes, Webb for Harmon after 63 minutes, Lyon not used

Scorers: tries – Forster (2), Gregory; goals – Woods (2)

Wigan: Hampson; Gill, Stephenson, Lydon, Russell; Edwards, Andy Gregory; Case, Kiss, Wane, Goodway, Potter, Hanley

Substitutes: Bell for Stephenson after 24 minutes, West for Wane after 53 minutes, Wane for Potter after 63 minutes

Scorers: tries – Gill, Hanley (2), West; goals – Stephenson, Lydon (5)

Referee: G. F. Lindop (Wakefield)

Attendance: 20,087

THE JOHN SMITH'S YORKSHIRE CUP

Leeds's first-round match against Hull was not just the most remarkable game of the whole competition, it was sheer melodrama. It engaged the spectators' emotions, it had reverses of fortune and it had a larger-than-life main character in Lee Crooks, who supplied the Leeds fans with a happy ending. Playing in the first half as if he could not overcome his regret at leaving Hull, he seemed to brace himself in the second half to lead Leeds from 6–24 down to an astonishing 28–24 victory, scoring a try, laying on two more and kicking six goals. The result had perhaps gone according to expectations but Hull, like many other underdogs, were left thinking, 'If only . . .'

After that bane of cup competitions, the preliminary round, in which Huddersfield were given a cruel draw at the Boulevard, and Wakefield had unconvincingly disposed of Dewsbury in a scrappy, sometimes violent game, the first round proper held few surprises. The scale of Bramley's 39–12 win over Doncaster was one of them, although they had beaten the same opponents in a league match ten days before. Elsewhere things went much according to form, but many of the losers could see in Hull's performance at Headingley something of themselves. Keighley, for example, almost upset Halifax, before the first-division club pulled ahead in the last quarter. Mansfield, the only non-Yorkshire team in the competition, appeared to be in control over York, until the well-practised craft of substitute Nigel Stephenson changed the course of the game. In another all-second-division tie, Featherstone found Batley hard work and then, well into the second half, Deryck Fox's individualist try set them on the way to a 28–6 win. Bradford's game at Hull KR, difficult to predict, ended in a 19–12 away win. Only Castleford, among the first-division teams, won in comfort, defeating Hunslet 32–12. The remaining match of the round, between Wakefield and Sheffield, followed a pattern like several others, with Sheffield looking better organised and altogether keener for two-thirds of the game until Trinity's experience took them through by a flattering 32–18 margin.

Trinity were on the receiving end of a similar experience in the second round at Leeds, where they were only 4 points behind after an hour's play. Among their four recent signings from Leeds, Mark Conway was outstanding, but the loss of their player-coach, David Topliss, upset their rhythm and they went down 8–36. For Featherstone, Deryck Fox was again the inspiration, scoring three tries in the 43–6 win over York. Bradford overpowered a plucky Bramley side by 30–6. The Halifax–Castleford game, however, with both sides having shown indifferent form, was a different matter. After an early Castleford lead, the match increased in intensity in the last quarter as Castleford absorbed all Halifax's pressure to win 10–0.

As in the previous season, Castleford went on to beat Featherstone in the semi-final. Holding a slender half-time lead they stepped up the pace to win 36–8. Bradford, who had lost in the semi-final the year before, repeated a recent league performance in defeating Leeds by 16–5. Their two former Leeds props, Jeff Grayshon and Brendan Hill, were outstanding. Their clash with Kevin Ward and John Fifita was expected to be one of the features of the final.

Headingley,
Leeds,
17 October

The Yorkshire Cup Final
Bradford Northern 12 Castleford 12

Castleford started their third successive County Cup final as they finished – showing plenty of attacking potential without being able to despatch a determined Bradford side. Though Bradford opened the scoring with a Keith Mumby penalty goal, Castleford always seemed the more likely to penetrate. This they did when John Joyner put Roy Southernwood into a gap and then Kevin Ward made a good break, but the attacks did not come to fruition. Then, when the referee was making the forwards pack down for the third time at the same scrum, loose forward Bob Lindner cleverly switched positions with David Roockley. The ball came from the scrum to Joyner, Lindner burst on to his pass from the full-back position and moved the ball wide to David Plange, but the winger's pass back inside was a poor one. Shortly after, Plange was again involved as he swept up Joyner's pass on the half-volley and went through Simpson and Francis to score at the corner flag and put his team ahead.

It is perhaps strange that Castleford, one of the major areas for producing Rugby League talent, should need to sign Australians, but Lindner showed his worth on several occasions, as did Michael Beattie and John Fifita. Directly from the restart the loose forward made a powerful run of over fifty yards, though Bradford's cover was equal to it. Lindner was eventually rewarded when, taking Joyner's pass, he forced his way over to give Castleford a deserved half-time lead.

Bradford made two changes at half-time: David Hobbs and Neil Roebuck took the place of Jeff Grayshon and Terry Holmes respectively. Castleford's hooker, Kevin Beardmore, was injured just before half-time and replaced by Dean Sampson. When his twin brother, Bob, came on after fifty-five minutes and scrum-half Roy Southernwood went to hooker, the Castleford forwards and half-backs were disrupted again. Whether the substitutions affected the outcome is uncertain, but what became quite apparent was that Bradford were beginning to assert themselves more and more, with the eventual man of the match, Paul Harkin, having a particularly busy afternoon.

The Bradford Northern scrum-half, Paul Harkin, won many admirers during the season for his wily skills. Nominated the man-of-the-match in the Yorkshire Cup final, he led his team to victory in the replay.

Bradford soon equalised: Karl Fairbank must have been surprised at the slackness of the marking as he went on a strong twenty-yard run from acting half-back to score a converted try. Hobbs then kicked a penalty to put Bradford 12–10 ahead, which Ketteridge matched seven minutes later. The score remained at 12–12 for the last fifteen minutes, but amid the increasing errors there were two nice touches. Grayshon, who had returned, broke and slipped the ball to Mumby, who, however, was unable to regather his own kick ahead. Then Lindner, less prominent in the second half, perhaps because of a facial injury, showed the kind of skill the British like to think is their own preserve: his quick burst and back-flick pass was as neat as anything you are likely to see, but, like so much else, it came to nothing and Castleford were left to ponder on the chances missed.

Bradford Northern: Mercer; Ford, McGowan, Simpson, Francis; Mumby, Harkin; Grayshon, Noble, Hill, Skerrett, Fairbank, Holmes

Substitutes: Hobbs for Grayshon and Roebuck for Holmes, both at half-time, Grayshon for Hill after 68 minutes

Scorers: try – Fairbank; goals – Mumby (2), Hobbs (2)

Castleford: Roockley; Plange, Marchant, Beattie, Hyde; Joyner, Southernwood; Shillito, Kevin Beardmore, Ward, Ketteridge, Fifita, Lindner

Substitutes: Sampson for Kevin Beardmore after 38 minutes, Bob Beardmore for Shillito after 55 minutes

Scorers: tries – Plange, Lindner; goals – Ketteridge (2)

Referee: K. Allatt (Southport)

Attendance: 10,829

Elland Road, Leeds, 31 October

The Yorkshire Cup Final Replay
Bradford Northern 11   Castleford 2
Two weeks is a long time in Rugby League. Bradford's Jeff Grayshon had broken his leg and a dejected Terry Holmes had gone off into retirement. Castleford also had cause to regret not being able to settle the Headingley final. Kevin Beardmore and Bob Lindner were still suffering from injuries they had received then; and the immediate reaction of their chairman to the unusual weekend replay had been to regard the scheduled home league fixture against Wigan as financially more rewarding and therefore more important. By the end of the game they had further cause for regret.

The first half turned out to be an untidy affair, characterised by many handling errors, largely forced by the weight of the tackling. If Bradford's forward power had been less dominant than expected at Headingley, they were keen to assert themselves now, though for Castleford John Fifita and Dean Sampson, who replaced him, relished the challenge more than most. But there was also a good deal of puerile pushing and shoving at the play-the-ball, as well as an increasing sense of frustration among the Castleford pack in particular. Brendan Hill, who was proving difficult to handle, then crashed over the line, scattering several would-be tacklers, in the manner of a former Bradford prop, Colin Forsyth. Castleford's only reply was a Martin Ketteridge penalty goal.

As the half-time hooter sounded, what seemed like a minor incident brought notoriety to the whole proceedings. Wayne Heron was tackled by Joyner and appeared to kick out in the tackle. Joyner took exception, others suddenly took an interest, soon to be joined by yet more. It was brief, but it was a brawl and Mr Allatt was left with the impossible task of trying to sort things out. At the restart, Joyner and Fairbank were sin-binned as a token punishment. Several days later the Rugby League's management committee, who had seen too much of this kind of thing already, imposed fines on as many culprits as they could identify, though Fairbank was cleared.

The second-half football was more open, but the defences still dominated. Castleford brought back Fifita in place of Southernwood and later on Giles Boothroyd replaced Keith England and though both replacements were individually sound, the overall effect was unsettling, as Joyner shuttled between stand-off and loose forward and the front row and second row were rarely the same from one scrum to the next.

After Phil Ford went close to the Castleford line, David Hobbs dropped a goal to put Bradford 5–2 ahead. Ford was then involved in the decisive moment. Finding himself in midfield in the Castleford '25', he passed the ball out unsuccessfully, regathered and went wide before passing inside to Heron who had a simple job to score. Hobbs converted, and with only three minutes left Bradford brought the curtain down on what remained of Castleford's aspirations.

Bradford Northern: Mumby; Ford, McGowan, Mercer, Simpson; Stewart, Harkin; Hobbs, Noble, Brendan Hill, Skerrett, Fairbank, Heron

Substitutes (not used): Redfearn, Roebuck

Scorers: tries – Hill, Heron; goal – Hobbs; drop-goal – Hobbs

Castleford: Roockley; Plange, Marchant, Beattie, Hyde; Southernwood, Bob Beardmore; Ward, Kenny Hill, Fifita, Ketteridge, England, Joyner

Substitutes: Sampson for Fifita after 19 minutes, Fifita for Southernwood at half-time, Boothroyd for England after 65 minutes

Scorer: goal – Ketteridge

Referee: K. Allatt (Southport)

Attendance: 8,475

The Rodstock War of the Roses County of Origin match ended in a third successive win for Yorkshire, this time by 16–10. Yorkshire were coached by Peter Fox of Featherstone Rovers, jubilant after the win. *Above*, Ellery Hanley is seen eluding the Lancashire defence, with his centre, Tony Marchant, in support. *Below*, Andy Gregory, the Lancashire scrum-half, passes out of the scrum.

SIX

Five Players of the Season

Trevor Watson

Once again the task of selecting five 'Players of the Season' proved to be exacting, thought-provoking and intriguing. Big names readily sprang to mind and this season in particular there was a temptation to pick more than one player from the same club. But a personal view is that this is too easy a way out and choices should be shared around, even though a couple of players have been omitted who would be on many supporters' lists of the top five.

Considerable pleasure came from sifting the various names and only afterwards did it strike home that, for once, no Australian had been chosen, even if a New Zealander had earned selection. Maybe there is a hidden meaning in this. The final choice consists of players whose performances at least gave me special pleasure during the season and made the game so much easier to write about and those who have worked consistently well in the best spirit of the code. As before, the choice is a purely personal one, made in the hope that it will lead to healthy discussion about the game.

SHANE COOPER (ST HELENS)

One of the main reasons for the impressive mid-season surge of St Helens, including victory in the final of the John Player Special Trophy, was unquestionably the form of their New Zealand stand-off Shane Cooper. Cooper played a few games at scrum-half when Neil Holding was injured but was at his best at No. 6 and his coach, Alex Murphy, was quick to make him captain. The Kiwi was never the quicksilver, flamboyant type of stand-off but was thoughtful, reliable and, in his quiet way, superbly effective.

It was remarkable, when checking back on a try-scoring move, how often it had developed from Cooper being in the right place at the right time. On numerous occasions matters seemed to be on the point of breaking down when Cooper appeared to make the all-important link and set things going again.

He was never really acknowledged as a try-scorer, but when he did cut loose it was impressive as he collected a record-equalling six for the club in the runaway win over Hunslet, ironically his first tries in the championship. Cooper's final tally of eleven tries in twenty-one matches was in no way a reflection on his impact on attack during his stay with Saints.

Cooper also used his intelligence as a footballer to play a valuable role in defence. He had the knack of being able to cover on the wings as well as being a highly effective stopper down the middle.

Shane Cooper was a superbly efficient half-back for St Helens. Alex Murphy was quick to make him captain and to a large extent it was the New Zealander's inspired form that brought the John Player Cup to Knowsley Road and helped them to third place in the final championship table.

Steve Hampson was easily the best full-back in the country during the 1987–88 season and it was a tragedy that a broken arm not only ruled him out of a Wembley cup final for the third time but denied him a place in the Lions' tour of Australasia.

Brendan Hill had an impressive season for Bradford Northern and developed into a prop-forward of real authority, playing in every match. Many thought him unlucky not to be included in the Great Britain party for Australasia.

STEVE HAMPSON (WIGAN)

The Wigan full-back, Steve Hampson, earned nationwide sympathy when a broken arm ruled him out of Wembley for the third successive time. He then won total admiration for the way he accepted that dreadful twist of fate and set about maintaining the spirits of his colleagues during the build-up to the Challenge Cup final. That alone would have earned him nomination as a player-of-the-year but Hampson also earned a flood of accolades for his skilled and courageous play to be readily accepted as the best full-back in the country by some distance.

Hampson produced a series of outstanding displays in big matches. His ability to take the high ball under pressure spread confidence throughout the team and he was always quick to turn defence into attack. He had an uncanny ability to gather a rolling ball at speed, even in the worst conditions, that few other players, let alone full-backs, could approach. He was equally brave with his tackling and developed an almost telepathic understanding with his club half-backs, Shaun Edwards and Andy Gregory, that enabled them to produce some classic tries out of nothing. Hampson's tour selection was such a matter of course that no other full-back was even named initially.

Wigan seem certain to reach Wembley again during his career. When they do, justice would be served by putting this extremely talented player into cotton wool and preserving him for the final appearance he so richly deserves.

BRENDAN HILL (BRADFORD NORTHERN)

When the Great Britain tour party was announced, there was considerable surprise that the list did not contain the name of the prop-forward, Brendan Hill. It was a measure of the respect he had earned during the season that the surprise was expressed as much in Lancashire as around Odsal. The season was one which saw Hill mature considerably. He developed from a roly-poly front-row man into a player of authority and accepted that there was far more to his job than simply bash and barge. Before the season began he had weighed more than 19½ stone but he trimmed down to under 18 stone without losing strength, and this proved ideal.

Odsal is not the best of grounds for a prop to play most of his rugby, but Hill showed exceptional mobility for a big man and stood up well in severe tests against the best front-row men around. He settled at No. 10 for Northern and despite his heavy involvement he played in every match for his club during the season. He ran hard and often and was difficult, not to say downright awkward, to stop as he rolled all over tacklers.

Hill made an impact with his running and then looked for his support and grew more adept at slipping the ball away from the tackle. Although he missed the tour, Hill has time to develop further and can make a big impact in every way on the future international scene.

Martin Offiah, who exploded into
Rugby League from Rosslyn Park
Rugby Union club, was the most
talked-about player of the season.
He broke Widnes's try-scoring
record, finished with forty-four
tries in all matches, and his
searing pace on many occasions
for the Lions impressed even the
Australian crowds.

Throughout the domestic season,
and later with the Lions in
Australasia, Roy Powell never
gave less than a totally committed
performance. He was chosen the
Leeds player-of-the-year and
should gain more honours during
1988–89.

MARTIN OFFIAH (WIDNES)

Winger Martin Offiah proved one of the most fascinating newcomers that the Rugby League code has welcomed for some considerable time. A masterly Widnes signing from Rugby Union, he survived the cultural shock of changing from one Park – Rosslyn – to another – Naughton – and within a matter of weeks had become the most talked-about player in the game.

Possessing blinding pace, Offiah showed a finishing ability that helped lift the Chemics clear of the rest. There was a good deal of disappointment after his debut for Great Britain in France, not an auspicious one, that he was omitted from the return at Headingley. His presence would have put at least 1,500 on the gate.

Perhaps too much was made at times of Offiah's so-called weaknesses and not enough of his strengths. His popularity was shown in the Premiership final, for there was a roar from the 35,000 fans every time the ball seemed likely to reach him. After his hat-trick of tries against St Helens which virtually clinched the title for Widnes, Alex Murphy commented in the Saints programme: 'I felt the only difference between the sides was Martin Offiah, who had a truly magnificent game. He showed us all how to run with the ball and take the chances that came his way.'

It is difficult to argue with that assessment and the beauty of it is that Offiah is still really a learner and there could be a great deal more to come.

ROY POWELL (LEEDS)

For some time the 23-year-old Roy Powell has been one of the unsung heroes at Leeds, a player very much taken for granted despite his impressive stature and Frank Bruno-like appearance. During 1987–88, he steadily gained recognition with a series of consistent, sometimes outstanding, performances.

Powell has a big heart to match his frame but improved as a footballer week by week. He was another young forward to appreciate the need to make the break and then make the ball available for the support; sadly, he often held the ball out in vain. Perhaps he suffered from the fact that he is not a demonstrative type of player, and much of his best work, particularly on defence, either went unnoticed or was simply accepted as normal.

It was not until the John Player final that his ability was fully appreciated and in that game he came very close to the man-of-the-match award for a display that included far more breaks than any other player on view. When the tour squad was named and players inevitably began missing matches for a variety of reasons, Powell plugged away for Leeds and missed only one match during the season and that was because he was on duty with Great Britain in France.

His wholehearted efforts were eventually recognised by the Headingley supporters when he was voted the first Englishman for four seasons to become the Leeds player-of-the-year. In a side that contained many big names and six tourists that was no mean feat.

SEVEN

The Amateur Game

Ron Girvin

Maurice Oldroyd, the national administrator of the British Amateur Rugby League Association, sat down after the BNFL National Cup finals had wound up the season in May, and declared: 'Today was the best finals day we have ever had.' He might just as well have said that about the whole season. It is fifteen years since BARLA was born, and progress has been steady ever since. But last season everything seemed to accelerate on and off the field, as BARLA continued with its aim to make amateur Rugby League a truly national sport by the centenary year in 1995. Vital decisions were made off the field: the colts battle with the Rugby Football League came to an end; the last remnants of the RFU barrier were dismantled; and a national development officer was appointed.

On the field there were reports from all over the country of improving standards of play. Perhaps the real yardstick came in the National Cup finals when Leigh Miners and Wigan St Patrick's respectively lifted the Youth Cup and the open-age National Cup in record-breaking style. Both performances were packed with pace, flair and splendid tackling. Leigh Miners ended Ellenborough's hopes of becoming the first Cumbrian team to lift the BNFL National Youth Cup with a 50–8 win. The margin surprised many people because nine of the Ellenborough side were beaten finalists the previous year. Clearly experience counted for little.

The game was a personal triumph for the Miners' full-back, Sean Tyrer, son of Colin Tyrer, who was in Wigan's Wembley side in 1970 and is now assistant coach to the current champions, Widnes. Sean, who played at Wembley for Wigan Under-11s in 1982, scored three tries and landed five goals to walk away with the man-of-the-match award. The young Miners side showed an amazing maturity in their play as they had the game sewn up in the first seventeen minutes, scoring no fewer than four tries. In all they got ten, the others coming from their skipper, Neil Disley, Mark Sarsfield, Andrew Candlin, Andrew Robinson, Qumar Ali, John Maxwell and Shaun Hodgkiss. John Bode scored both Ellenborough tries in a purple patch just after half-time.

Wigan St Patrick's amazed everyone by getting anywhere near the National Cup final. In two seasons in the National League, they finished wooden spoonists and had won more games in this one competition than in those two seasons in the league. The second shock came in the final, when they came back from 6–8 down at half-time to turn on a brilliant exhibition to topple Elland 28–8. It left Wigan hailing yet another win over Halifax . . . following the professionals' triumph at Wembley.

St Patrick's long-serving chairman, Cliff Fleming, claimed that the post-

Christmas return of Martin McLoughlin and Conal Gallagher had made all the difference and it was easy to see why. McLoughlin linked up from full-back superbly to split the Elland defence time and again as St Patrick's moved the ball wide. To crown it all, Gallagher, who has been studying law at Hull University, scored one of the finest tries seen in any final. There he was, a 16-stone prop with bags of pace, breaking through in his own half like a threequarter, kicking past Elland's full-back and regathering to score. What a try! St Patrick's other tries came from David Jones (2), Paul Unsworth and the veteran Frank Priest, with George Winstanley kicking four goals. Skipper Dave Fairbank and Martin Taylor scored tries for Elland, who had knocked out the holders, Thatto Heath, in the semi-final.

St Patrick's triumph meant that teams in the National League had failed to pick up only one of the major trophies, the Cumbria Cup. It was a point that the League chairman, David Knight, was quick to seize upon at the annual dinner. 'The standard of play in the National League this season has shown a considerable improvement and a gap is clearly developing between this League and others. New standards are being set,' he said proudly, and continued that in 1989–90 the League is to have two divisions.

Milford became champions of the National League under the guidance of Allan Agar. Allan picked up a Challenge Cup winners' medal with Hull Kingston Rovers, and then led Featherstone Rovers, as coach, to one of the biggest ever Wembley upsets when Hull were the victims.

In this their championship year, Milford enjoyed a winning sequence of thirteen victories on the trot, after suffering two defeats in the opening four games. However, they failed to pull off a double by taking the newly inaugurated Slalom Lager Challenge Cup. That went to a rejuvenated Leigh Miners, who beat Milford 15–0 in the final at McLaren Field, Bramley, on a dreadful April Sunday afternoon. Rain was lashing down throughout the game and there were pools of water on the pitch.

The match will probably be remembered best for a brilliant third try by the Miners centre, Peter Marsh. Taking the ball thirty yards out, he skipped across the mud, swerved past three defenders, and finished up between the posts to leave himself with an easy goal kick. The Miners stand-off, Steve Grimshaw, had put them in front with a drop-goal, before their second-rower, Wayne Lee, crashed in for a try, and then Shaun Unsworth polished off a splendid move with a second touchdown. The man-of-the-match award went to the 19-year-old Miners prop-forward, Mike Williamson, and how well he deserved it for his non-stop effort in the conditions. Milford just couldn't contain the lively Miners pack although they probably missed the presence of their loose forward, Richard Milner, who won so many man-of-the-match awards. What pleased Miners most about the win was that they did it without veterans John Cooke and John Webster.

The teams that day were as follows:

Leigh Miners: Simpkin; Pilling, Marsh, Unsworth, Hunt; Grimshaw, Burke; Williamson, Dowling, Balmer, Lee, Sutton, Casey

Substitutes: Smith, Cooke

Scorers: tries – Lee, Unsworth, Marsh; goal – Marsh; drop-goal – Grimshaw

Milford: Turner; Schofield, Buckle, Binder, Thacker; Hannah, Miller; Monks, Morrow, Barker, Hill, Toulson, Johnson

Substitutes: Ellis, Sheldon

Referee: C. Morris (Huddersfield)

It must have been some consolation that, a week after the final, Milford finally overtook Pilkingtons in the race for the League title. They also beat Miners 41–8 in a League clash. Pilkingtons, under the former Great Britain and St Helens international, John Mantle, set a tremendous pace as they dropped only one point in their first nine games. But they faltered badly in the second half of their programme, picking up only 7 points from nine games.

The difference in league and cup form for Leigh Miners was remarkable. They had to settle for a mid-table spot in an inconsistent season but, when it came to cup football, they were a totally different proposition. Apart from lifting the National League Cup, they had earlier in the season crushed Farnworth 22–4 in the Burtonwood Brewery Lancashire Cup final. The Widnes side never really competed, which was surprising in view of the fact that they had knocked out Pilkingtons and Crosfields.

Kells picked up the Cumbria Cup for the fifth time in six years with a 36–7 win over Wath Brow. Amazingly, Wath Brow led 7–6 at the interval. Playing in their sixth Bass Yorkshire Cup final, West Hull toppled Ace 21–4 to lift the trophy for a fourth time. With the reigning champions, Heworth, being exempt, these county cup results meant that the National League had three teams through to the preliminary round of the Rugby League Challenge Cup. And once again the amateurs showed that they fully deserved to be back in the big time with the professionals. Heworth and West Hull were paired together and the York side triumphed 11–4 to set themselves up for a crack at the Challenge Cup holders, Halifax, only to be crushed 4–60 before an all-ticket crowd of over 3000.

Kells attracted a crowd of 5,874 for their midweek tie with mighty Leeds, who included the Great Britain Test centre, Garry Schofield, among their array of stars. It was the biggest crowd to pack into the Whitehaven ground since 1972 when Whitehaven met Salford in a Lancashire Cup semi-final. It also bettered the 1986–87 gate of 3,665 for a John Player Trophy tie between Whitehaven and Leeds. Although Kells finally lost 0–28, all the neutrals agreed that Leeds had had to work hard for their five tries.

It was a similar case at Hilton Park, where Leigh Miners were defeated 23–4 by Hunslet, a somewhat flattering scoreline. Mind you, Hunslet didn't see much of the ball as Tony Dowling won the scrums 3–1 to take the man-of-the-match award, and played his heart out in the loose. Earlier in the season, the 1986–87 National Cup finalists, Heworth and Thatto Heath, figured in the John Player Trophy. Heworth went down 32–5 to Swinton, while Thatto Heath put up a tremendous performance against Featherstone Rovers, before a couple of late tries gave Rovers a 34–16 margin. Those ties provided something of an ironic twist for the former St Helens star, Frank Barrow. Frank had guided Heath to their National Cup success the previous season and was with

Wigan St Patrick's celebrate their triumph in the final of the BARLA National Cup, sponsored by BNFL, by 28–8 against Elland of Halifax.

them as they tried to knock out the professional side. The following day, in his role of assistant coach at Swinton, he was there again trying to ensure that the amateurs were knocked out.

One success against professional opposition came from the Shape Engineering North-west Counties side, Crosfields. Along with the league champions, Thatto Heath, Crosfields played in the Lancashire Shield competition with the professional clubs' 'A' teams, something that had never happened previously. In fact Crosfields caused a bit of embarrassment as they knocked out Widnes 'A' and Carlisle 'A', before being beaten in the semi-final by the eventual winners, Warrington 'A'. Everyone agreed that the entry of the amateurs had added spice to the competition.

It was a busy season on the international front with a second visit from Papua New Guinea and a first trip for the Junior Kiwis. Papua New Guinea played only one game against the amateurs, edging home 20–16 against a BARLA XIII. BARLA led 10–6 at one point thanks to a try from Paul Messenger and three Tom Brook goals, but the tourists came back to 20–10 before Steve Critchenson got the second try and Brook his fourth goal. The main object of the Papuans' trip was a World Cup clash with Great Britain and several games against the professionals. Considering that the tourists defeated Featherstone Rovers and drew with Lancashire, the BARLA side won for themselves a good deal of credit.

Having been thrilled by the performances of the Young Kangaroos the previous year, a lot was expected of the Junior Kiwis, and we weren't disappointed. They included a big strapping 6ft 2in, 15st centre, hailed as the new

Mal Meninga. His name was Kevin Iro, and he soon showed why he had earned such rave notices. Scoring tries came easily to him and it was not surprising that, after helping another touring side, Auckland, he signed for Wigan and played for them in the Challenge Cup final picking up two of the first three tries with his brother Tony getting one.

In an Under-19 Test, Great Britain didn't do too badly against them. Injuries to the Great Britain winger, Steve O'Connor, and the scrum-half, Shaun Lang, disrupted them badly in the first Test at Elland Road, and they went down 8–30. But they played better in the second Test at Wigan, with the Kiwis being pressed all the way before winning 21–10. St Maries' brilliant half-back, Chris Kelly, got all Britain's points with a try and three goals in the second Test. He also landed three goals in a 6–12 reverse against France, in Toulouse, and his performance in those two internationals won him the BARLA young player-of-the-year award. The equivalent open-age award went to the Ace Amateurs forward, Steve Critchenson, for a second successive year. Steve, who has played in twenty-six Tests, turned in top-class displays against Papua New Guinea and in a 16–0 win over France at Whitehaven. It was Great Britain's first home win over the French for six years.

The Queensbury forward, Basil Richards, set that game alight after a scoreless first half, ripping holes in the French defence and picking up one of the tries. The others came from Steve Ostle (Ellenborough) and Bob Jowett (Dudley Hill), with Thatto Heath's Tony Pennington kicking two goals. After that game Maurice Oldroyd was given a medal of honour by the French Rugby League Federation for his services to the game, a splendid and well-deserved honour.

Happenings off the field were as important as those on it during 1987–88. The wrangles over the Rugby Union barrier and the Colts League were settled at last, with more than a little help from the Sports Council. BARLA and the RFU finally agreed on a free gangway between the codes which meant that amateur players could move from one code to the other without being banned. There was a lot of happy co-operation between amateur Rugby League and Union clubs and the two London League finals were staged at Wasps Rugby Union ground in Sunbury, something no one could have dreamed about even a couple of years ago. The RFL and BARLA finally agreed on a joint de-velopment scheme which meant an end to the controversial Colts League. To support the development of the game, the Rugby League Foundation, a charitable trust, came into being. An Irishman, Tom O'Donovan, was named as the first national development officer and he took office determined that BARLA could claim by 1995, the centenary year of Rugby League, that the game was truly a national one. To help him, the appointment of several new development officers was announced: Ian Harris will work on Humberside; the former New Zealand Test forward, Kevin Tamati, in Warrington; Trevor Gibbons in Leeds; Tim Butcher in South Yorkshire; and Niel Wood in Rochdale.

There have been signs throughout the season of the game gaining in popu-larity in the South-West, the Midlands, London and the North–East. And we even had a Welsh and Scottish Universities match as a curtain-raiser at Knowsley Road. There is no doubt that Amateur Rugby League is thriving.

The John Player Special Trophy

Preliminary round	1st round	2nd round	3rd round	Semi-finals	Final
	Springfield B 14 / Barrow 2	Springfield B 14 / Wakefield T 8	Springfield B 12 / Leeds 22	Leeds 19 / Wigan 6	Leeds 14 / St Helens 15
York 38 / Bramley 2	Wakefield T 22 / York 22 (Replay: 30–6 to Wakefield T)				
	Whitehaven 14 / Leeds 18	Leeds 20 / Halifax 10			
	Halifax 32 / Keighley 6				
Heworth 5 / Swinton 32	Swinton 12 / Salford 18	Salford 14 / Dewsbury 5	Salford 12 / Wigan 16		
	Dewsbury 14 / Doncaster 12				
	Wigan 34 / Sheffield E 8	Wigan 26 / Castleford 16			
Featherstone R 34 / Thatto Heath 16	Featherstone R 12 / Castleford 34				
	Carlisle 16 / Warrington 22	Warrington 12 / Hull KR 8	Warrington 10 / Oldham 14	Oldham 8 / St Helens 18	
	Hull KR 30 / Rochdale H 12				
	Batley 18 / Hunslet 16	Batley 0 / Oldham 44			
Oldham 36 / Fulham 8	Oldham 22 / Bradford N 6				
	St Helens 12 / Widnes 10	St Helens 40 / Mansfield M 0	St Helens 20 / Hull 16		
	Runcorn H 4 / Mansfield M 6				
	Hull 42 / Workington T 6	Hull 19 / Leigh 7			
	Leigh 28 / Huddersfield 12				

The John Smith's Yorkshire Cup

Preliminary round	1st round	2nd round	Semi-finals	Final
	Bramley 39 / Doncaster 12	Bramley 6 / Bradford N 30	Bradford N 16 / Leeds 5	Bradford N 12 / Castleford 12 (Replay: 11–2 to Bradford N)
	Hull KR 12 / Bradford N 19			
Hull 54 / Huddersfield 8	Leeds 28 / Hull 24	Leeds 36 / Wakefield T 8		
Wakefield T 25 / Dewsbury 14	Wakefield T 32 / Sheffield E 18			
	Featherstone R 28 / Batley 6	Featherstone R 43 / York 6	Featherstone R 8 / Castleford 36	
	Mansfield M 18 / York 23			
	Halifax 34 / Keighley 12	Halifax 0 / Castleford 10		
	Castleford 32 / Hunslet 12			

Appendix 3

The Grünhalle Lager Lancashire Cup

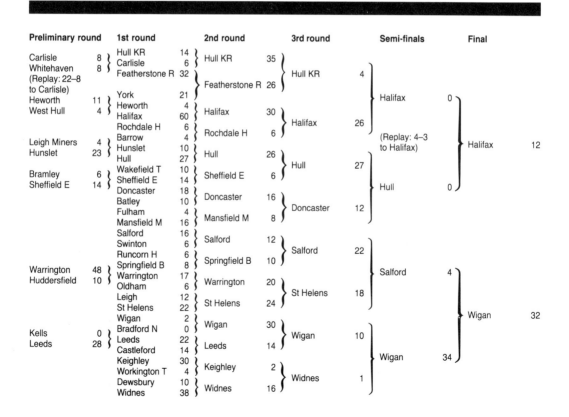

1st round		2nd round		Semi-finals		Final	
Workington T	12	Workington T	10				
Springfield B	10			Warrington	44		
Warrington	42	Warrington	50				
Oldham	8					Warrington	16
Swinton	38	Swinton	22				
Rochdale H	20			Swinton	6		
Leigh	27	Leigh	14				
St Helens	21						
Whitehaven	28	Whitehaven	14				
Carlisle	12			Widnes	12		
Runcorn H	6	Widnes	20				
Widnes	40					Wigan	28
Barrow	2	Wigan	42				
Wigan	36			Wigan	20		
Salford	58	Salford	2				
Fulham	4						

Appendix 4

The Silk Cut Challenge Cup

Preliminary round		1st round		2nd round		3rd round		Semi-finals		Final	
Carlisle	8	Hull KR	14	Hull KR	35						
Whitehaven	8	Carlisle	6			Hull KR	4				
(Replay: 22–8		Featherstone R	32	Featherstone R	26						
to Carlisle)								Halifax	0		
Heworth	11	York	21								
West Hull	4	Heworth	4	Halifax	30						
		Halifax	60			Halifax	26				
		Rochdale H	6	Rochdale H	6			(Replay: 4–3		Halifax	12
Leigh Miners	4	Barrow	4					to Halifax)			
Hunslet	23	Hunslet	10	Hull	26						
		Hull	27			Hull	27				
Bramley	6	Wakefield T	10	Sheffield E	6			Hull	0		
Sheffield E	14	Sheffield E	14								
		Doncaster	18	Doncaster	16						
		Batley	10			Doncaster	12				
		Fulham	4	Mansfield M	8						
		Mansfield M	16								
		Salford	16	Salford	12						
		Swinton	6			Salford	22				
		Runcorn H	6	Springfield B	10						
Warrington	48	Springfield B	8					Salford	4		
Huddersfield	10	Warrington	17	Warrington	20						
		Oldham	6			St Helens	18				
		Leigh	12	St Helens	24						
		St Helens	22							Wigan	32
		Wigan	2	Wigan	30						
Kells	0	Bradford N	0			Wigan	10				
Leeds	28	Leeds	22	Leeds	14						
		Castleford	14					Wigan	34		
		Keighley	30	Keighley	2						
		Workington T	4			Widnes	1				
		Dewsbury	10	Widnes	16						
		Widnes	38								

The Stones Bitter Championship
Final League Tables

Division 1

	P	W	D	L	Points F	A	Pts
Widnes	26	20	–	6	641	311	40
St Helens	26	18	–	8	672	337	36
Wigan	26	17	2	7	621	327	36
Bradford Northern	26	18	–	8	528	304	36
Leeds	26	15	3	8	577	450	33
Warrington	26	14	2	10	531	416	30
Castleford	26	13	–	13	505	559	26
Halifax	26	12	–	14	499	437	24
Hull Kingston Rovers	26	11	1	14	420	480	23
Hull	26	11	–	15	364	595	22
Salford	26	10	–	16	368	561	20
Leigh	26	9	–	17	416	559	18
Swinton	26	4	2	20	390	780	10
Hunslet	26	4	2	20	363	779	10

Division 2

	P	W	D	L	Points F	A	Pts
Oldham	28	23	1	4	771	335	47
Featherstone Rovers	28	21	2	5	712	353	44
Wakefield Trinity	28	20	1	7	666	315	41
Springfield Borough	28	18	–	10	448	356	36
Sheffield Eagles	28	16	1	11	490	429	33
York	28	15	1	12	558	526	31
Mansfield Marksman	28	15	1	12	439	412	31
Keighley	28	15	–	13	497	428	30
Barrow	28	14	2	12	382	397	30
Workington Town	28	15	–	13	380	441	30
Carlisle	28	14	1	13	388	446	29
Runcorn Highfield	28	14	–	14	420	469	28
Whitehaven	28	10	1	17	417	452	21
Bramley	28	10	1	17	400	600	21
Dewsbury	28	10	–	18	417	519	20
Doncaster	28	9	2	17	406	512	20
Fulham	28	10	–	18	382	559	20
Rochdale Hornets	28	10	–	18	322	514	20
Huddersfield	28	7	1	20	383	597	15
Batley	28	6	1	21	305	523	13

Appendix 6

The Stones Bitter Premiership

1st round		Semi-finals		Final	
St Helens	40	St Helens	24	St Helens	14
Castleford	8				
Bradford Northern	32	Bradford Northern	10		
Leeds	18				
Widnes	36	Widnes	20	Widnes	38
Halifax	26				
Wigan	12	Warrington	10		
Warrington	24				

Second Division

1st round		Semi-finals		Final	
Oldham	34	Oldham	18	Oldham	28
Keighley	24				
Springfield Borough	11	Springfield Borough	10		
Sheffield Eagles	10				
Featherstone Rovers	42	Featherstone Rovers	20	Featherstone Rovers	26
Mansfield Marksman	1				
Wakefield Trinity	44	Wakefield Trinity	16		
York	23				

Appendix 7

Leading Scorers

Tries

Offiah (Widnes)	44
Hanley (Wigan)	36
Schofield (Leeds)	25
Gibson (Leeds)	24
Goodway (Wigan)	23
Pape (Carlisle)	23
Edwards (Wigan)	21
Foy (Oldham)	21
Smith (Featherstone Rovers)	21
Bibb (Featherstone Rovers)	20
Conway (Wakefield Trinity)	20
Elia (St Helens)	20
Quirk (St Helens)	20

Goals

Woods (Warrington)	152
Quinn (Featherstone Rovers)	128
Harcombe (Wakefield Trinity)	116
Loughlin (St. Helens)	114
Pearce (Hull)	111
Smith (Springfield Borough)	98
Stephenson (Leeds)	95
Fletcher (Hull KR)	94
Hobbs (Bradford Northern)	83
Jones (Salford)	79

Points

	Trs	Gls	Dr.-gls	Pts
Woods (Warrington)	13	147	5	351
Quinn (Featherstone Rovers)	11	127	1	299
Loughlin (St Helens)	8	114	–	260
Harcombe (Wakefield Trinity)	3	116	–	244
Pearce (Hull)	6	102	9	237

2

The Great Britain Whitbread Trophy Tour of Papua New Guinea, Australia and New Zealand, May–July 1988

Garry Schofield, seen here playing for the
Chairman's XIII against Auckland at
Headingley, was desperately unlucky to have
to join the throng of injured players making
their way home from the Lions' tour of
Australasia. Schofield played in only five
matches, scoring five tries, before his
cheekbone was fractured in the match against
a Combined Brisbane XIII.

The Great Britain Whitbread Trophy Tour of Papua New Guinea, Australia and New Zealand, May–July 1988

Ray French

When the Rugby League Council announced that Dr Forbes Mackenzie would be the first doctor to accompany a Great Britain tour to Australasia they must have been blessed with psychic powers or the craft of a fortune-teller, such were the medical problems and complications which were to frustrate the preparations of the coach, Mal Reilly, between the naming of the tour party on Tuesday 5 April and their departure for Papua New Guinea on Monday 16 May. Indeed, it was actually found impossible to name a twenty-six-man squad when the tour management met the media at Rugby League headquarters in Leeds. The announcement of only twenty-three players and the provision for a 'train on' squad of ten highlighted circumstances which proved almost farcical as the time for take-off drew near.

It was difficult to counter those sceptics who doubted Britain's chances of success when, for example, the Leeds prop, Lee Crooks, who was selected for the 'train on' squad, had not played a full match for five months after complications with a dislocated collar-bone; the wing, Des Drummond, was struggling to regain fitness after knee ligament trouble; and Kevin Beardmore was about to undergo surgery for a depressed cheek bone.

Within weeks, Wigan's outstanding second row, Andy Goodway, had pulled out of the tour for business reasons and the Lancashire club's brilliant full-back, Steve Hampson, had suffered the cruel blow of a broken arm. Crisis talks among the management were further aggravated when two of Great Britain's most experienced players, Drummond and Lydon, were withdrawn from the party. Dr Forbes Mackenzie was certainly 'on call', if only to hand out tranquillisers to the beleaguered management team.

Nevertheless the inclusion of Roy Haggerty (St Helens), Hugh Waddell (Oldham), and Ian Wilkinson (Halifax) did ensure that a party of twenty-four players, smartly clad in tour uniform, left the Bentley Arms, Leeds, for Heathrow Airport, with Carl Gibson, the Leeds winger, and Andy Platt, the St Helens second row, still suffering from ankle ligament trouble, due to depart the following week. The party was made up as follows:

Manager	Les Bettinson
Coach	Malcolm Reilly
Assistant coach	Phil Larder
Business manager	David Howes
Doctor	Dr Forbes Mackenzie
Physiotherapist	Geoff Plummer

95

The Great Britain Whitbread Trophy Tour

Players

Kevin Beardmore (Castleford)	Roy Haggerty (St Helens)
Brian Case (Wigan)	Ellery Hanley (Wigan) (captain)
Lee Crooks (Leeds)	David Hulme (Widnes)
Paul Dixon (Halifax)	Paul Loughlin (St Helens)
Shaun Edwards (Wigan)	Paul Medley (Leeds)
Karl Fairbank (Bradford Northern)	Martin Offiah (Widnes)
Michael Ford (Oldham)	Andy Platt (St Helens)
Phil Ford (Bradford Northern)	Roy Powell (Leeds)
Carl Gibson (Leeds)	Garry Schofield (Leeds)
Henderson Gill (Wigan)	David Stephenson (Leeds)
Andy Gregory (Wigan)	Hugh Waddell (Oldham)
Mike Gregory (Warrington)	Kevin Ward (Castleford)
Paul Groves (St Helens)	Ian Wilkinson (Halifax)

To join the party on 17 June   Steve Hampson (Wigan)

Though planned to be one of the shortest Great Britain tours, the itinerary suggested that it would be one of the most demanding with Britain expected to play only eighteen matches in nine weeks but faced with five Test matches against Papua New Guinea, Australia, and New Zealand, three of which, against each country, were to be World Cup qualifying matches. The manager, Les Bettinson, was honest enough to admit that it was a formidable task for a squad lacking so many of the original first-choice selections. 'The past month has been a traumatic experience,' he said. 'Our best laid plans were ruined and many unpredictable things have happened. But perhaps these nightmare experiences will be good for us on tour.'

Such chaotic preparation was certainly not the best start for a tour which was of crucial importance to the future of British Rugby League and for a team striving to win the Ashes for the first time since 1970. However, Les Bettinson confidently declared that, 'We have assessed the ability, personality traits, adaptability, and responses to pressure of the players we have selected.' But, despite all the physical, psychological, and mental preparation, the question on everyone's lips was whether Great Britain could mount a serious challenge abroad with the limited rugby ability now remaining at coach Mal Reilly's disposal.

With an average age of only twenty-four years, and with only six previous tourists in the squad, Mal Reilly and his assistant coach, Phil Larder, had collected together, in their opinion, a good blend of youth and experience. In midfield much was expected of the Wigan half-back combination of Shaun Edwards and Andy Gregory, whose performance at Wembley only a fortnight before departure, gave rise to hopes that the days of Alex Murphy and David Bolton or Tommy Bishop and Roger Millward were to return. The man-of-the-match display of David Hulme of Widnes in the Premiership Trophy final also augured well for Britain's strength at half-back. Garry Schofield, with his unique try-poaching ability and his five tries in the 1986 Ashes series, surely would pose a threat while the captain, Ellery Hanley, the first coloured player to be awarded the honour of captaining a Lions team abroad, had the ball skills and the physical prowess to dominate matches. In Martin Offiah and Phil Ford there was no shortage of pace, though there must have been questions raised over the quality of their defence in the heat of Test rugby. In the forwards, Lee Crooks and Kevin Ward were props who had competed with the best in Australia on many occasions.

I believed the Lions had the nucleus of a sound Test team, able to mount a competitive Ashes challenge, if all played to form and if the squad kept relatively free from injury. However, the reserve players in the party were far short of Test standard. The lack of a true ball-playing forward, apart from Lee Crooks, cast doubts on the pack's ability to break up the ferocious defensive unit of the Kangaroos' midfield. The lack of real size in many of Britain's forwards worried me too after our failings in this department during the 1984 Lions tour and remembering the size of the forwards to be met in Australia and, especially, in New Zealand. The loss of Steve Hampson, at least until after the first Test against Australia (as was hoped, though in the event Hampson never recovered sufficiently to leave Britain), meant that against Papua New Guinea and in the early games in Australia our last line of defence would have to be entrusted to a novice at international level.

Though I had misgivings with regard to a selection policy which could only take notice of two players, Martin Offiah and David Hulme, from Widnes, the Stones Bitter champions, Mal Reilly was adamant that the squad had been selected with a specific purpose in mind and was quietly confident of their ability to carry out the task. 'The team has been selected for its ability to run all day, support each other, and be fit. Provided we can build on our team spirit and attain the correct attitudes then I am confident we can spring a surprise on them,' Reilly said.

The skipper, Ellery Hanley, was also eager to underline his coach's viewpoint when he insisted that, 'We are an adaptable squad with players able to play in many positions', but the traditional pre-tour sparring between the Lion and the Kangaroo really began in earnest when the former Australian Test prop, Les Boyd, in a sensational newspaper article, declared, 'I don't hold out much hope for Reilly's lot. The Aussies will take them apart. No way will this series be competitive.' My head urged me to nod in agreement with Les Boyd but my heart advised me to put my trust in Mal Reilly.

The coach must have been relieved that he put his trust in Dr Mackenzie for, without his advice and experience, there is little doubt that the Lions would not have started the tour with such a convincing victory as they achieved by 42–22 against Papua New Guinea in the Test. And he had every reason to be well satisfied by the disciplined approach of his players who, when faced with the doctor's prescription for success, appreciated that, whatever strictures were enforced, were in their best interests. A ban on alcohol and an appeal to drink water at regular intervals, as a guard against the possibility of dehydration, was introduced to counteract the intense heat and humidity in Port Moresby. Sleeping tablets, to overcome jet lag after a forty-hour flight, and regular coolings with wet towels, were prescribed for the players throughout the three days prior to kick-off. And by the time kick-off arrived it was a decidedly nervous squad who arrived at the tiny Lloyd Robson stadium.

The Kumuls coach, Skerry Palanga, buoyed by their victory over a Brisbane XIII earlier in the week, was confident of his team beating the Lions and had flown his full-back, Dairi Kovae, from the North Sydney club in Australia to strengthen his side. With an estimated 12,000 crowd packed into the stadium, many having arrived as early as 9 a.m., and with others perched in the branches of nearby trees or hanging from pylons, the welcome for Great Britain might possibly have proved overwhelming for one or two of the younger players, especially when the Mud Men of Asaro performed their ritual dance before the match in a most intimidating manner.

In such an atmosphere and faced with such hostile climatic conditions it was only natural that Mal Reilly should select his most experienced team, his only gamble being the inclusion of the St Helens 21-year-old centre, Paul Loughlin, at full-back. That Great Britain won well was due to a combination of sound medical research and the players' determination to overcome the odds stacked against them by launching an all-out assault on the Kumuls' try-line at the beginning of the match.

Port Moresby, 22 May (World Cup qualifying match)

Papua New Guinea 22 Great Britain 42

Despite the sorry departure from the field, after only seven minutes, of Shaun Edwards, suffering from a twisted knee, three tries from Garry Schofield, Paul Medley, and Henderson Gill plus two goals from Paul Loughlin in the opening eleven minutes established a handy 16-points lead and a cushion against the heat later in the match. Even the further loss of the prop-forward, Brian Case, in the thirty-fourth minute with a knock above the eye failed to upset the rhythm of the tourists' attacks, invariably led by their dynamic scrum-half, Andy Gregory, who revelled in the extra responsibility placed on his shoulders by the loss of his half-back partner, Edwards. A scoreline of 28–6 in the Lions' favour at half-time would normally be sufficient cause for relaxation on the management's part but not when the game is played beneath the burning sun of Papua New Guinea. And especially when, as Les Bettinson the manager explained, chaos reigned in the dressing-room at half-time. 'Some of the players could not breathe. David Stephenson was physically sick and the whole team had red faces and were completely drained.'

In that torrid final forty minutes the Kumuls siezed the initiative with tries from Arnold Krewanty and Dairi Kovae, his second of the match, and when prop Isaac Rop raced through Kevin Ward's tackle to score beneath the posts, Bal Numapo landed the third of his goals to bring them within 8 points of victory and to a slender scoreline of 30–22 in Great Britain's favour.

Thankfully David Stephenson recovered from his half-time exertions sufficiently to take advantage of a perfectly timed Garry Schofield pass and veered inside to score. Henderson Gill made victory safe when he added a second try in those vital five closing minutes and young Paul Loughlin crowned a competent display in his unaccustomed position of full-back with his seventh goal. Great Britain had to be grateful to Ellery Hanley for his try-saving tackles and to the forwards, Kevin Ward and Mike Gregory, for their wholehearted efforts but Mal Reilly, though delighted with the win, confessed that, 'We gave away some silly points but we can improve a hundred per cent.'

Papua New Guinea: Kovae; Krewanty, Morea, Numapo, Saea; Haili, Kila; Bom, Malmillo, Rop, Kombra, Evei, Kovoru

Substitutes: Rombuk for Bom after 59 minutes, Lapan for Kombra after 77 minutes

Scorers: tries – Kovae (2), Krewanty, Rop; goals – Numapo (3)

Great Britain: Loughlin (St Helens); Ford (Bradford Northern), Schofield (Leeds), Stephenson (Leeds), Gill (Wigan); Edwards (Wigan), Andy Gregory (Wigan); Ward (Castleford), Beardmore (Castleford), Case (Wigan), Medley (Leeds), Mike Gregory (Warrington), Hanley (Wigan)

Substitutes: David Hulme (Widnes) for Edwards after 7 minutes, Paul Dixon (Halifax) for Case after 34 minutes

Scorers: tries – Schofield (2), Gill (2), Medley, Mike Gregory, Stephenson; goals – Loughlin (7)

Referee: G. McCallum (Australia)

Attendance: 12,000

Great Britain could feel well pleased with themselves after beating a Highland District XIII 36–18. Martin Offiah continued his highly successful first season in League by registering a hat-trick of tries and Mal Reilly was comforted by the fact that the prop, Lee Crooks, came through his first full match for five months unscathed. The news that Shaun Edwards had flown directly to Sydney to receive specialist treatment on his injured knee gave cause for concern and alarm that he might be forced to withdraw from the tour before the remainder of the party had even arrived in Australia.

Then the announcement that the Widnes centre, Darren Wright, had been asked to fly out to join the party made the news surrounding Edwards's knee look even more ominous. Thankfully, the suggestion after the operation, that Edwards might be fit to resume after about three weeks put the party in good spirits for the third match of the tour against North Queensland at Cairns. The squad were in even better spirits when they registered the highest score for twenty-six years by any touring side in beating North Queensland by 66–16. Martin Offiah again proved what a lethal force he could be if properly used, with a further four tries whilst the nine tries scored by the team in the second half stemmed from the free flowing patterns of play that Reilly was trying to instil into the team in these country matches. On the following Sunday the players deserved their snorkelling adventure on the Great Barrier Reef but it was back to three strenuous days of training when the Lions arrived in Sydney to prepare for their first major test on Australian soil – against the Newcastle Knights.

That training, indeed the match preparation throughout the tour, was excellent and there was always an air of real professionalism about Reilly's and Larder's arrangements. Twice daily training, the first at the unearthly hour of

8 am and often carried out at the nearby Manly Rugby Union club, was always strenuous, varied, and impressive in its attention to detail. Few tricks were missed even to the extent of using Australian balls in practices and, from the routine stretching exercises, through to the vigorous physical sessions and the crisp passing routines there was an eagerness to work hard. The players responded well, with the captain, Ellery Hanley, often being left to take the final session himself. The handling especially, before the Newcastle game, was impressive, with only Les Bettinson, the manager, dropping a pass in a one-hour session.

In the team's hotel overlooking the golden sands of Manly beach, notice-board displays featuring possession counts, tackle counts, penalties incurred, daily itineraries and match reports were displayed prominently. At the end of the corridor Dr Forbes Mackenzie and the physiotherapist, Geoff Plummer, transformed a large suite of rooms into a doctor's surgery. The players could ask for no better treatment or leadership and, despite a few hiccups, they responded against the Newcastle Knights.

In the absence of the injured Shaun Edwards, Ellery Hanley was selected in the stand-off position but Reilly made clear what was required of him. 'I want Hanley to play an orthodox game; otherwise I shall have to consider others and put him back at loose forward.' With Garry Schofield falling foul of the stomach bug that suddenly hit camp, the new arrival, Darren Wright, was plunged into his first match.

Newcastle,
NSW,
1 June

Newcastle Knights 12 Great Britain 28

Andy Gregory proved to be the architect of this confidence-boosting win with a display that indicated his growing maturity. After fifty-five minutes the score was delicately balanced at 12 points each and all the good play of the first half, when Kevin Ward and Martin Offiah had scored tries and Paul Loughlin had added two goals to give the Lions a comfortable 12–4 lead, was squandered. The old failings of a Great Britain side, lapses in defence, too slow around the rucks, and an inability to take chances, allowed the Knights to roar back with three tries from Greg Shore, Tony Kemp, and Glen Miller.

The home crowd bayed for a win but, thankfully, the Lions showed far greater resilience and commitment in their tackles with the second row of Mike Gregory and Paul Dixon recording no fewer than sixty-eight tackles between them and with the hooker, Kevin Beardmore, able to monopolise the scrums. At last Kevin Ward looked to have found the form he showed when playing for Manly but it was Gregory and Hanley who finally sealed the Knights' fate.

Hanley used his upper body strength to shrug off two tackles in a solo dash to the try-line and Andy Gregory laid on two other tries, one for Martin Offiah, his ninth of the tour after only three match appearances, and one for Hanley after a scrum break. The overall performance was rather like the curate's egg, good and bad, but, in Martin Offiah and Paul Loughlin, who caught the ball well at full-back and ran with determination at every opportunity, Reilly had two worthy Test candidates. Life had stirred in the British Lion and the win was important in the face of a critical and at times hostile Australian press. But Mal Reilly himself insisted, 'There is still much to do. Our defence has got to move up even quicker.'

Sadly the quiet satisfaction at the win was shattered the next day by the news that, after a further visit to see Merv Cross, Australia's leading sports injury consultant, Shaun Edwards was advised to return home as quickly as possible. Manager Les Bettinson, devastated by the further loss of an established Test player, summed up his feelings philosophically when he remarked, 'You play the cards from the hand that you are dealt.' The next two matches against Northern Division at Tamworth and against Manly would determine, among other positions, who would be the new Test stand-off.

In their drama, the ancient Greeks believed that when tragedy was enacted on stage then the Gods took a hand and expressed their sympathy with a blast from the heavens. The gathering of clouds and the freak thunderstorm which shrouded the tiny Tamworth ground in darkness and gloom at the final whistle captured the sense of despair and a disaster of tragic proportions. The scoreline of 36–12 in Northern Division's favour was cruel humiliation for the British players as they trooped from the pitch. Mal Reilly's remark, after the Newcastle match, that there was 'much to do' returned to haunt him in a game which proved the pack's work rate to be an embarrassment, the defence to be virtually non-existent and the experiments of playing David Hulme at stand-off and Lee Crooks at prop to be hardly conclusive, though in Crooks's case it was, in a negative way.

Despite Hulme's high tackle count he was ineffective on attack, possibly suffering from the pathetic efforts of the pack in front of him, while Crooks's performance only served to highlight the glaring deficiencies in his physical fitness after such a long lay-off. It was already apparent after this disgraceful result, the biggest defeat outside the Tests in Australia for sixty-eight years, that the 'ham and eggers' section of the touring party would, unless strengthened by seasoned Test players, struggle against even moderate opposition.

There was little optimism about the possibility of a win, two days later, against the Sydney Premiership winners, Manly, when Mal Reilly continued his policy of sheltering his best players – Andy Gregory, Schofield, and Hanley – from the hurly burly of the minor matches and reserving them for the first Test.

Manly,
Sydney,
7 June

Manly 30 Great Britain 0

As the bedraggled British players left the pitch at the end of what proved to be a battering from the huge and powerful Manly pack, a shrewd observer of many tours abroad wondered whether signs of life in the Great Britain squad had been finally extinguished. Indeed, after registering yet another 30 points defeat, without reply, it looked as if Mal Reilly would need superhuman powers to revive his team's chances of success in the Ashes series. And yet, though he was prepared to concede that, 'Manly are a formidable side, well drilled and well organised,' he stressed once again that, though concerned at the result and the inadequacies of the reserve squad, he supported his single-minded policy that, 'Our mission is to win the Ashes.'

An opening twenty minutes of loose passes, indiscipline at the rucks, and slack defence allowed Manly's rampant giants, Noel Cleal and Mark Pocock, to assert such relentless forward pressure on the Lions' try-line that two tries by their forwards Ian Gateley and Pocock effectively put paid to Great Britain's hopes of a win. When Manly's tiny eighteen-year-old scrum-half and man-of-the-match, Geoff Toovey, raced over for a further try Britain were once again facing another humiliation before a good sized crowd of 11,131 who had every reason to demand their money back, such was the lack of competition for the home club.

Test candidates David Hulme and David Stephenson worked hard at half-back, especially in defence, while the loose forward, Andy Platt, was the pick of the pack, his tackling doing much to restrict Manly to a further two tries from Charlie Haggett and Cliff Lyons and two goals from Tim Dwyer to complement his three in the first half. The substitution of the prop, Lee Crooks, late in the game gave the French referee, Francis Desplas, a few hectic moments when a flurry of fists erupted and he was forced to dispatch Roy Haggerty and Manly's Mark Brokenshire to the sin-bin for five minutes. Alas, this was to be Britain's only impact, albeit a physical one, on a night when it was patently obvious that, after only six games on tour, the reserve grade players were simply not good enough to tackle any Australian side without the assistance of half a dozen of the Test squad. The manager, Les Bettinson, acknowledged this, and even before preparations began for the first Test, it was agreed that such weak sides would not be fielded in future.

That the Test team picked itself was obvious even to the most casual observer, with the result that, when Mal Reilly announced his side on the Wednesday evening before the game, the only surprise was the inclusion of Halifax's Paul Dixon in the unlikely position of prop. The coach had stuck to his plan to field a highly mobile pack and Dixon, with his tigerish tackling, pace, and high work-rate fitted the bill, though it was a gamble to put him against players the size of Australia's Sam Backo and Phil Daley. David Hulme, too, must have been surprised to be given the daunting task of facing Australia's captain, Wally Lewis, at stand-off but he had earned his first Test cap by his application over the past month.

The recriminations of the previous two defeats were forgotten and training began for the Test squad on the Thursday morning, ironically at the sun-drenched Brookvale Oval, the scene of the team's disaster against Manly. In fact, they had begun their preparations under the guidance of the assistant coach, Phil Larder, nine days before when he had occupied them in aerobic running. Long runs, often along the beach, were combined with visits to a weights gymnasium to encourage strength and endurance. The others were given a huge psychological boost when, having managed only runs of 2×8 lengths of the pitch every thirty seconds in Papua New Guinea, their fitness was such that they were now able to complete 3×10 runs of the pitch with only thirty-second intervals. More intense anaerobic work, in which each player, even the prop, Kevin Ward, ran 10×200 metres in under thirty seconds, was accomplished until the sessions were gradually wound down to short thirty-yard sprints. During all this time, over five days, work with the ball at set piece play and tactical discussions were held until, with the slackening of training on the Thursday and Friday, all the squad were placed on a carbohydrate diet to aid their energy factor. Such is the scientific preparation for a modern rugby Test.

Nothing had been left to chance by the management but the question still to be answered was whether the players could actually match Australia, the world champions and undefeated in the past thirteen Tests against Great Britain. The Kangaroo coach, Don Furner, thought that Britain could match his side in skill but doubted their commitment. 'The Poms are as skilful as we are but whether their commitment to defend and work hard for each other is there, remains to be seen.' We would not know the answer until the end of the centenary Test and the first to be played on Sydney's new 60-million dollar football stadium.

Australia fielded five new caps in Andrew Ettingshausen, Peter Jackson, Tony Currie, Phil Daley, and Sam Backo and many critics expressed doubts about the strength of the pack without such established Test stars as Wayne Pearce and Noel Cleal. But few were prepared to bet against them, despite bookmakers being prepared to give Great Britain a 15-points start.

Sydney,
11 June
(First Test)

Australia 17 Great Britain 6

At half-time, the Australian coach, Don Furner, decided to ask his scrum-half, Peter Sterling, to return to the field from which he had been led only ten minutes before, clutching his left shoulder in considerable pain. This decision proved the turning point of a magnificently fought centenary Test match. Sterling had made a gallant effort in the thirty-eighth minute to stop Great Britain's captain, Ellery Hanley, racing in for a try at the corner of the right-hand touchline, only to fall awkwardly on the point of his shoulder as he made his despairing dive. Hanley shrugged off Sterling, rounded the covering Bob Lindner and swept past Garry Jack with contemptuous ease. Britain, deservedly, were ahead 6–0, and Sterling, the destroyer of Britain's hopes throughout the 1980s, was leaving the field. The 'pop-gun poms', as they were labelled in Sydney, were suddenly firing too many big guns for the Kangaroos, who retired to their dressing-room shell-shocked.

Those opening forty minutes will be stamped indelibly on the minds of the vast number of British supporters seated around the Sydney Football Stadium. Great Britain had roared back out of the Test match wilderness and announced to a sceptical Australian public that the Kangaroos' crown as world champions was in danger. With a well planned kicking game the Lions had kept Australia in their own half with long punts downfield from Paul Loughlin who, despite missing four out of five goal attempts, enjoyed a fine Test match debut, running the ball well out of defence and invariably beating the first couple of tackles. Garry Schofield and Andy Gregory broke up the tight Australian defence with grubber-kicks that sliced through at angles to the touchlines and gained thirty or forty yards. Australia were forced to retreat for the first time since the power game of the Australian packs erupted onto British shores in 1982. It was Great Britain who had the power and the ideas.

The Castleford forward, Kevin Ward, following his ritual before the Sydney Grand Final in 1987, when he played for Manly, bathed in the sea off the Manly beach at 7.00 a.m. on the morning of the Test. The much vaunted Australian props, Sam Backo and Phil Daley, must have regretted that those predatory creatures which haunt the Australian shoreline, the sharks, hadn't taken an interest in British beef as they floundered around the pitch like

After a typically
powerful and
elusive run,
Great Britain's
captain, Ellery
Hanley, touches
down to put
Britain in the
lead in the first
test in Sydney.

Great Britain's
prop, Kevin
Ward, showed
an appetite for
Australian
conditions. His
ability to link
with Andy
Gregory, despite
in this case the
attentions of
Wally Lewis and
Greg Conescu,
was a feature of
the Tests.

beached whales in Kevin Ward's wake. Ward burst through tackles at will, passed the ball, usually to his club colleague, Kevin Beardmore, ever in support, and caused a spate of Australian mishandling with the ferocity of his tackling. His front-row colleague, Paul Dixon, also showed little respect for his more experienced opposite number, Phil Daley, and he and a tremendously fit and enthusiastic back-row trio of Andy Platt, Mike Gregory and Ellery Hanley on more than one occasion sent Australia back twenty or thirty yards with a series of 'big hits' as the Aussies like to call powerful tackles. At half-time, Australia were booed from the pitch by a section of the crowd; Great Britain walked to their dressing-room with heads held high. But they hadn't bargained on the bravery of Peter Sterling, the genius of Wally Lewis, and the evident shortcomings of the French referee, Francis Desplas.

Britain's second-row forward, Mike Gregory, showed great commitment among a determined Lions' pack. His runaway try in the third Test will long be remembered, though here he is held by the Australian full-back, Garry Jack, in the first Test.

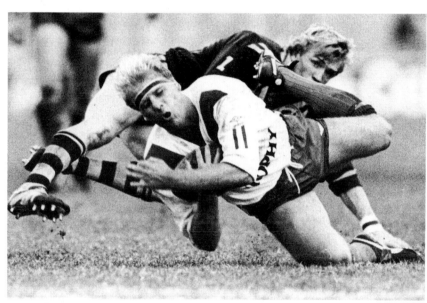

Blood, sweat, toil, and eventually tears, are not enough to win matches against this modern Australian team when confronted with this sort of half-back pairing of Sterling and Lewis. Their feats rank with any partnership in the history of Rugby League; indeed, I have never seen a better half-back pairing. Their genius is truly unique, their understanding uncanny. Their impact on the second half of this first Test was, once again, to prove devastating to British hopes.

In the forty-ninth minute Sterling's misdirected grubber-kick was quickly regathered on the rebound from a British player and, with lightning reflexes, the ball was quickly transferred to the big prop, Sam Backo, who, despite the attentions of Ellery Hanley, forced his way over for a try. O'Connor converted and the match was evenly balanced at 6–6. Sixteen minutes from the end Sterling again, after concerted Australian attacking play, held up the final pass for Peter Jackson to sprint through a gap to give Australia the lead for the first time at 12–6. With Lewis and Sterling spraying out passes in all directions the

Australian attack began to look menacing at last. Lewis sensed victory with a drop-goal from the Great Britain 25-yard line before he and Lindner combined to send Jackson over for his second try and certain victory for Australia by the flattering margin of 17–6.

In my opinion, the referee played an important part in the Kangaroo victory with his inconsistent decisions which frequently broke up play and halted many British attacks. His attitude to infringements seemed a casual one. He kept the ball in Australian hands, prior to their opening try, for longer than necessary by waving play on after mythical British hands had supposedly touched the ball and after a blatant knock-on by an Australian player at a play-the-ball. Such extensions of pressure on Great Britain's defence eventually took their toll.

Though the Lions restored their reputation as worthy candidates in Test rugby the sad truth is that in the end they lost the match by their own shortcomings. If only Kevin Ward's pass had not been ruled forward when Andy Gregory scampered over the try-line half way through the second half. If only Paul Loughlin had not missed four out of five kicks at goal. If only Garry Schofield had not knocked the ball on, twice, as he sped for the try-line. If only the Lions had not allowed Australia to escape the pressure when on their try-line in the second half, through indiscipline and back chat to the referee. And above all: if only Peter Sterling had stayed, injured, in the dressing-room at half-time.

However, Great Britain did at last show that they had the power, speed and fitness to match the mighty Australian machine that for the past ten seasons has appeared invincible. After an impressive pack performance Kevin Ward, the man-of-the-match and the recipient of the sponsors' $1000 award, was moved to say, 'Our pack has broken through a psychological barrier. We had them on the run and beat an Australian pack at its own game.' Others, too, had impressed the Australian public and proved the right to join the long list of heroes who have worn the red, white, and blue colours and battled bravely in Sydney. Andy Gregory was a menace to Australia throughout the match. This tough, aggressive character inspired his side with a stream of long passes to enable his threequarter line to operate smoothly, and his short passes helped the forwards to pierce holes in the Australians' defence. His half-back partner, David Hulme, distributed well, made a couple of slicing breaks in midfield and, certainly at the set pieces, kept Lewis under control. On the wing, Phil Ford proved most elusive and excelled with piercing, darting runs which relieved pressure on the British line and often set up counter-attacks. In contrast, though Offiah proved an exciting runner when in possession, his experience at Test level led to him dancing inside far too much, causing a great deal of confusion to his colleagues.

At the final whistle there was sadness and despondency in the Great Britain dressing-room as they contemplated 'the one that got away'. Mal Reilly declared, 'We made too many mistakes when in good attacking positions and lost our rhythm with our kicking gone in the second half.'

The Australian coach, Don Furner, declared, 'I've been saying since the Lions arrived that they were never going to be easy and this afternoon they showed just how much respect they deserve to have from the Australian team.'

That respect and the stirring British performance meant that despite those inglorious defeats at Tamworth and Manly, the appetite of the Australian public had been so whetted for Test rugby again that all eyes were now turned to the eagerly awaited clash in the second Test at Lang Park, Brisbane.

Australia: Jack; Ettingshausen, O'Connor, Jackson, Currie; Lewis, Sterling; Backo, Conescu, Daley, Fullerton-Smith, Vautin, Lindner

Substitutes: Folkes for Vautin after 70 minutes, Belcher for Sterling after 75 minutes

Scorers: tries – Backo, Jackson (2); goals – O'Connor (2); drop-goal – Lewis

Great Britain: Loughlin (St Helens); Phil Ford (Bradford Northern), Schofield (Leeds), Stephenson (Leeds), Offiah (Widnes); David Hulme (Widnes), Andy Gregory (Wigan); Ward (Castleford), Beardmore (Castleford), Dixon (Halifax), Platt (St Helens), Mike Gregory (Warrington), Hanley (Wigan)

Substitutes: Powell (Leeds) for Mike Gregory after 70 minutes, Gill (Wigan) for Loughlin after 78 minutes

Scorers: try – Hanley; goal – Loughlin

Referee: F. Desplas (France)

Attendance: 24,480

The city of Brisbane allows a touring party to relax a bit after the intense media examination of Sydney. Players swim, go sightseeing, or sail, free from constant public exposure. However, the Great Britain manager, Les Bettinson, stressed the need for four good wins in Queensland prior to the second Test if they were to rescue the trip from its precarious financial situation. The decision to field much stronger teams in the minor matches represented a deliberate change in policy by the management. But they could hardly have anticipated that more shattering blows were to hit them after only four days. First, Andy Platt, one of the successes of the tour, was ruled out for a couple of weeks with a badly bruised wrist and became a doubtful starter for the second Test; and worse was to follow against a combined Brisbane XIII at Lang Park.

Brisbane, 15 June

Combined Brisbane XIII 14 Great Britain 28

Seventy years ago, Lang Park was a cemetery. At 9 p.m. on Wednesday 15 June it was where British hopes of regaining the Ashes in 1988 were finally laid to rest. After twenty minutes of play, the world's costliest player, Garry Schofield, was led from the field with a fractured cheekbone. Within a week he was on his way home after an operation in Brisbane hospital. Then the scrum-half, Michael Ford, suffered a fractured left hand. Battling on in considerable pain throughout the match, he was later relieved to learn that he would have to miss only ten days of the tour. David Stephenson hobbled off the pitch with a knee injury and Brian Case received a gash above his left eye which needed eight stitches. This had been a catastrophic game. When added to the previous injury toll, the new wounded left only fifteen fit players available to fly to Rockhampton to face Central Queensland. A few of the Press contingent were even faking thigh strains so as to avoid selection! However, on the credit side, the Lions had won the game 28–14, Martin Offiah had returned to his best form with two tries, while the captain, Ellery Hanley, proved why he was such a threat to Australia in the Tests. His forceful and elusive running, allied to Phil Ford's opportunism at full-back, provided tries for Schofield, Fairbank, and Michael Ford. David Stephenson added four goals. A further encouragement for Mal Reilly was that the prop, Lee Crooks, came through another eighty minutes in his slow recovery to full fitness.

Not surprisingly the mood at breakfast the next morning was a sombre one. However, both Reilly and Les Bettinson did much to raise spirits dampened by the loss of Schofield and the other injuries. Instead of a hard training routine, a relaxing sauna and a swimming session at a local gymnasium proved a tonic for the players and a meeting between the management and such senior players as Ellery Hanley, Kevin Ward and Andy Gregory did much to unite the squad and fuel a determination to beat the obstacles stacked against them.

Now, however, they were faced with yet another disaster. The damaged disc at the base of Paul Medley's neck still gave the specialist cause for concern and he was advised to rest for a further six weeks, advice which meant that he too was to join the shuttle service of players returning home. However, coming in the other direction from Britain were the Widnes pair, Andy Currier, as replacement for Schofield, and Paul Hulme, brother of David, as cover for Medley. In truth, Paul Medley had not displayed the form which made him so devastating earlier in the season and I was one who felt that Paul Hulme might prove more than useful as a utility player. The inability of Lee Crooks to last more than seven minutes in the Rockhampton match against Central Queensland also proved a setback, especially when Les Bettinson announced that 'Lee is definitely out of the second Test.'

Further damage to the muscles of Crooks's right shoulder, the dislocation of which had given rise to many problems before the tour began, did not appear to cause the management undue alarm and, on the Saturday following the match against Central Queensland, Crooks was merely recommended a couple of exercises to strengthen the muscles. My own view was that Crooks, for all his determined efforts in training, would never play a full part in the 1988 tour and should have been replaced there and then. Surprisingly this fresh string of injuries, piling up on top of the Schofield disaster, did not dampen the spirits of the players who enjoyed an eleven-try romp at Rockhampton, none performing better than Martin Offiah, whose beautifully balanced running brought him a hat-trick of tries, and Ellery Hanley, who gained two tries from sheer opportunism. Karl Fairbank, having his best game of the tour helped himself to three tries, and Roy Powell deserved a try for his wholehearted efforts. The hot sun and the carnival atmosphere surrounding the annual cattle show at Rockhampton set the mood for the resounding win and the reward for the players of a trip to Surfers Paradise on the Sunday following the match.

With the growing injury list, the Lions' next two matches, at Toowoomba and against Wide Bay at Gympie, were a great worry to Reilly as he prepared for the second Test at Brisbane. Though he fielded a near full-strength team for the match at Toowoomba, his principal concern in both matches was to remain injury-free. Sadly, his hopes were not to be realised: both Ian Wilkinson and Stephenson, who fell heavily on his shoulder against Toowoomba, were injured.

In both matches, ruined by over-zealous referees who penalised Great Britain on every possible occasion, there was little to suggest that anyone outside the recognised Test team would challenge for a place. Phil Ford showed himself a capable candidate for the centre position in the absence of Schofield with a sound display and a well taken try at Toowoomba, while Andy Currier, who made his debut against Wide Bay, along with the other replacement, Paul Hulme, showed considerable pace when racing in for his try. Both wins meant that Mal Reilly's promise of four victories in Queensland had been achieved but none had been gained in such a convincing fashion that he could approach the next battle with Australia with any great confidence. Moreover, Andy Gregory's hamstring injury and Stephenson's bruised shoulder failed to respond to treatment as quickly as Reilly would have liked. Despite the Lions' excellent team spirit, and the gift by an Australian company of a magnetic-pulse-wave machine to aid the injured players' recovery, the Test team was in doubt as late as the Monday afternoon prior to the match.

The sight of a fully fit Andy Gregory racing around the Souths' club pitch on the eve of the Test did much to lift the spirits of the whole party. He was chirpy and cocky again, strutting up and down the training area, barking instructions at everyone and keeping his forwards on their toes. Sadly, David Stephenson failed his fitness test, causing Mal Reilly to move Ellery Hanley to the centre, along with Phil Ford, and to include the industrious Roy Powell at prop. Powell had earned his selection for his consistency in previous matches whilst Hanley's move to centre was made not only with the intention of plugging a gap left by the injured Stephenson but to ensure that his tackling ability would restrict Australia from playing a wide running game. The pack lined up as expected, though it was obvious from the grimaces on Andy Platt's face and the delicate way in which he protected his damaged arm that his only relief from the pain of his injury would be from a pain-killing injection. His selection was a gamble but, I think, a justifiable one if we were to achieve parity again in the forwards.

A brilliant blue sky greeted the tourists on the morning of the game but, as in all matches with an evening kick-off, the day passed slowly for the Test team and few wanted to take advantage of the sun. Former players, such as George Nicholls, Roger Millward, Phil Lowe and David Topliss, visited the hotel; many of the 2000-strong army of British supporters called to wish their favourite players well; but most of the squad kept to the privacy of their rooms. Pop music and endless TV programmes could be heard along the hotel corridors; the clinking of coins during the endless games of cards were an occasional distraction, but the day was really spent in contemplation of the events to come.

A fanatical Queensland crowd packed the Lang Park stadium. There was a

109

carnival-like atmosphere with the brilliant floodlights and firecrackers, the pitch like an immaculate green baize cloth spread out below. A crescendo of roars greeted the teams as they emerged from the dressing-rooms. With eight internationals missing from the original squad of twenty-six players there was a British bulldog spirit on the terraces. Below, now entering the arena, were fifteen Great Britain players with the words of Vince Lombardi, the famous American football coach, ringing in their ears, 'Winning isn't everything, but the will to win is everything.' We had the will but whether the next eighty minutes would give us everything was a debatable point at 7.35 p.m. when Paul Loughlin kicked off for the Lions.

Brisbane,
25 June
(Second Test)

Australia 34 Great Britain 14

By 9.15 pm when the match was over and Great Britain had been defeated by 14–34, it was clear that will power alone was not enough and that the failings of old – slack defence, indiscipline, and an inability to maintain possession for any length of time – were again in evidence. In a spiteful match, marred by flashes of ill-temper, especially from the Great Britain scrum-half, Andy Gregory, and Australia's prop, Sam Backo, and ruined by some disgraceful head-high tackling, the side that maintained their discipline was clearly going to win. Australia did just that and retained the Ashes for the fifth successive series. Despite an early lead from a Paul Loughlin penalty, Phil Ford's misdirected tackle on Michael O'Connor, which ultimately led to his try in the seventh minute, set the pattern for high tackling and a failure to put any real pressure on the Australians. That failure to exert real pressure or mount any consistent attacks was further heightened by the Lions' inability to retain possession for the full six tackles and their penchant for kicking the ball aimlessly into touch on the full.

When Australia retain possession for something like seventy per cent of a match then such is the pressure from their forwards that tries will inevitably come, especially with the genius of Wally Lewis behind the pack. His chip kick for Peter Jackson's try in the twentieth minute was perfectly placed, and seventeen minutes later he was to be the lynchpin of Ettingshausen's try. A pass from Australia's best forward, Sam Backo, two dummies from Lewis himself, a pass to Garry Jack, who distinguished himself with a couple of sorties from the back, and a try was a formality. With Sam Backo, Wayne Pearce, and Phil Daley proving difficult to stop in midfield and with Paul Vautin, in the second half, beginning to show his ball-playing skills, Great Britain were caught in a stranglehold. The ball was continually dropped, kicks by David Hulme, Paul Loughlin, and Andy Gregory were misdirected and for all the efforts of Paul Dixon, playing gallantly with a broken thumb, and Kevin Beardmore in the pack, it was only a matter of time before the onslaught began.

A brief moment of inspirational brilliance from Ellery Hanley, who raced through a gap on the right to combine with Phil Ford who scored beneath the posts, and a glimpse of Martin Offiah's blistering pace, when he rounded Garry Jack and Belcher to score, gave a glimpse of what Britain might have achieved had they adopted a more disciplined approach. Sadly those moments of delight for the British fans were punctuated by two tries from Backo and Pearce, both from close forward work, and a final flourish from Lewis who rounded off Bob

Lindner's thirty-yards break with a try. O'Connor nonchalantly brought his points tally for the match to 14 with his fifth goal.

Andy Gregory and Ellery Hanley occasionally proved dangerous runners but, heavily beaten in the forward battle, there was little cohesion in the British attack, and far too many players panicked when under pressure. In contrast, Australia needed only a workmanlike performance from their team and the guiding hand of the man-of-the-match, Wally Lewis, to go 2–0 up in the series. Mal Reilly offered no excuses, saying, 'I was expecting our forwards to give the same commitment as they did in Sydney but it wasn't there and the Australian pack took charge.'

Australia's captain, Wally Lewis, is brought to the ground by Paul Dixon, the Lions' second row, in the second Test in Brisbane after being knocked off balance by Roy Powell.

Australia: Jack; Ettingshausen, O'Connor, Jackson, Currie; Lewis, Sterling; Backo, Conescu, Daley, Fullerton-Smith, Vautin, Pearce

Substitutes: Lindner for Conescu after 68 minutes, Belcher for Ettingshausen after 74 minutes

Scorers: tries – O'Connor, Jackson, Ettingshausen, Backo, Pearce, Lewis; goals – O'Connor (5)

Great Britain: Loughlin (St Helens); Gill (Wigan), Phil Ford (Bradford Northern), Hanley (Wigan), Offiah (Widnes); David Hulme (Widnes), Andy Gregory (Wigan); Ward (Castleford), Beardmore (Castleford), Powell (Leeds), Dixon (Halifax), Platt (St Helens), Mike Gregory (Warrington)

Substitutes: Paul Hulme for Platt after 51 minutes, Wright for Phil Ford after 69 minutes

Scorers: tries – Phil Ford, Hanley; goals – Loughlin (3)

Referee: F. Desplas (France)

Attendance: 27,130

It is surely stretching the imagination too far to think that the mischievous spirit which seemed to haunt the 1988 tour intended 'Rule Britannia' to be played over the radio on the team bus as the party left Brisbane for the flight back to Sydney. Certainly the strains of the anthem failed to stir the players from their sombre mood, a mood induced by the realisation that they had, only the night before, pressed the self-destruction button on their Ashes hopes. Later that day, the regular medical bulletin, now beginning to rival *The Lancet* in its listing of interesting diagnoses and medical disasters, was to bring further bad news. Both Andy Platt (broken wrist) and Paul Dixon (broken thumb) were to return home and when, the next day, the management finally accepted the inevitable and instructed Lee Crooks to accompany them, the party, with six matches still to play, were forced, yet again, to fly out a couple of replacements. Richard Eyres (Widnes) and the experienced Test campaigner, John Joyner (Castleford), arrived in time to take their places against the President's XIII at Canberra.

A diversion concerning the accusations of head-high tackling from both sides in the second Test, and a move by the Australians to replace the French referee, Francis Desplas, caused some animosity between the two countries but, after a meeting called by the chairman of the International Board, Ken Arthurson, both coaches and managers eased the tension by agreeing to encourage the players to provide an entertaining spectacle in the third Test. However, there were still two difficult hurdles to be jumped by the Lions before then, at Orange against the Western Division and against the President's XIII in Canberra.

Britain reserved one of their worst performances of the tour for the quiet country town of Orange where, despite two thrilling tries from Martin Offiah and industrious performances from Hugh Waddell and Mike Gregory in the forwards, the efforts of many of the side almost drove Malcolm Reilly to despair. After some inept displays from the reserve players, which highlighted the paucity of talent once the injured Test players had been removed, Reilly could only stand in the dressing-room in disbelief after the game and declare, 'What can I say?' Happily he had more to say at the rain-sodden Seiffert Oval in Canberra when, though defeated 16–24 by a strong President's XIII, which included Test players of the calibre of Mal Meninga and the promising scrum-half, Greg Alexander, he had seen his side stage a tremendous fight back in the second half. Two long-range tries by the full-back, Phil Ford, and encouraging performances from Mike Gregory and Richard Eyres, playing in his first match on tour, helped to instil, yet again, a mood of quiet optimism within the squad. The only problem for Reilly, apart from the hair-raising flight back from Canberra to Sydney in one of the worst storms of the winter, was the injury to Kevin Beardmore in the tenth minute of the match. A badly bruised hip caused the Castleford hooker to hobble from the pitch in severe pain and he, more than any other player, was in need of the rest day given to the players, before preparing, on the Thursday, to have one last tilt at the Australians.

It says much for the morale of the Great Britain squad that there was a determined mood among both management and players as they set out for training sessions at the Penrith club but the search for a first Test win against Australia since 1978 was resembling a knight's search for the Holy Grail. Ever had it proven elusive, and there were few in Sydney who expected a Lions win, given the injury crisis and the performances since that memorable first Test.

Indeed, anyone wandering around Great Britain's training-area on the Friday morning must have felt that he had stumbled on a major disaster, so many were the bodies lying around the pitch. Mike Gregory lay sprawled, nursing an ice pack on his groin, Richard Eyres held a similar pack to his knee, Paul Groves hobbled alongside, stepping gingerly on a bruised big toe, and Andy Gregory searched for any telling twinges in his thigh as he tested his hamstring with stretching exercises. The Castleford front-row pair, Kevin Beardmore, ultimately to be ruled out with a severely bruised right hip, and Kevin Ward, suffering from a damaged ankle, sat alongside the fence surrounding the training pitch, their grim expressions betraying the sombre mood of the camp. By the afternoon training session Richard Eyres, too, had been declared unfit. Thus, in addition to Paul Hulme, who was to make his full Test debut as hooker, Hugh Waddell was deservedly picked to make his first Ashes Test appearance at prop. Though Malcolm Reilly declared that, 'The British bulldog is at its best when its back is to the wall', few can have imagined the dramatic events that were to unfurl over the next twenty-four hours. Certainly not John Hogan of *The Australian* who summed up the feelings of his fellow countrymen when he declared in his newspaper, 'Forget "Test" – this match is just a sham. The Lions are simply not good enough and will be forced to field a team which is not in the same class as their awesome opposition.' No doubt he and all those thousands of Australian Rugby League followers who shunned what was to prove an historic Test match will live to regret their lack of confidence in Great Britain's ability to defy all obstacles and, as in the 'Rorke's Drift' Test of 1914, emerge gloriously triumphant.

Sydney,
9 July
(Third Test
and World Cup
qualifying
match)

Australia 12 Great Britain 26
In the forty-second minute of this pulsating match, Wally Lewis, so often in the past Australia's inspiration at stand-off, shrugged off the attempted tackles of Paul Hulme and Hugh Waddell, resisted Phil Ford's outstretched arms and forced his way over for a brilliant solo try. Michael O'Connor kicked the first of his two goals and suddenly Australia had narrowed Britain's lead to 10–6. That comfortable half-time lead of 10–0 had evaporated and the thousands of British supporters who had waved their Union Jacks, blown their bugles, and roared their support at Phil Ford's and Martin Offiah's earlier tries suddenly had a sickening feeling in their hearts. Would all the glorious rugby and Britain's complete tactical command in that first half now be lost? A quick run-around move between Kevin Ward and Andy Gregory had resulted in Gregory's lobbed pass launching Offiah to the try-line as early as the sixteenth minute. And four minutes later the elusive Phil Ford, who taunted the Australians with his side-stepping runs throughout the match, darted into midfield from the left-wing position and weaved his way through a bemused defence. Loughlin's conversion had raised an extra cheer from the British camp, themselves

stunned at the ease with which the Lions had raced through the normally tight Australian defence. But would Lewis and his team now turn the tables on the Lions with their usual second-half onslaught? Happily, it was not to be, for, as skipper Ellery Hanley explained, 'When Lewis scored we knew it was the turning point of the game. We stepped up our play, crowded them out, and the match was ours.'

Within six minutes, the Lions had replied with the first of Henderson Gill's tries. Whether running, passing, or kicking the little scrum-half and man-of-the-match, Andy Gregory, was behind all Great Britain's attacks. His delicately placed chip-kick allowed Gill to race behind the covering Australian full-back, Garry Jack, and score. Loughlin added the second of his three goals and suddenly 'this was the stuff that dreams are made on'. Though big Sam Backo replied with a try for Australia, two pieces of individual brilliance and sustained running served to underline the almost total control which Great Britain had gained. The St Helens centre, Paul Loughlin, growing in confidence with every minute, burst through two tackles on the right-hand side of the field in his own 25-yard area and raced upfield with Henderson Gill in attendance. Though the pass to Gill was slightly early, the Wigan wing had no problem in rounding Garry Jack's despairing tackle to score at the corner.

Andy Gregory breaks past Tony Currie to set up another Great Britain attack in the third Test in Sydney.

Gill's grin and triumphant jig at the end of that 75-yard scoring movement expressed the elation of the British team. The skill, strength, and fitness of the side were never better illustrated than in their final try in the seventy-first minute, begun by Andy Gregory and completed in dramatic fashion by his namesake Mike. The chunky, fiery scrum-half sent the Australian defence the wrong way with an outrageous dummy, barely fifteen yards beneath his own posts. He raced through a gap and with his chest heaving and his little legs pumping he burst clear. Mike Gregory, the game's outstanding forward, raced alongside and, at the half-way line, received the ball with everyone expecting him to pass to the flying Martin Offiah at his side. Not so, as Gregory indicated his contempt for the fitness of this Australian side and his belief in his own speed. He outpaced Lewis and Pearce over fifty yards to the try-line as a forlorn Kangaroo side were left to stand back and admire.

David Stephenson throws out an unorthodox pass despite Fullerton-Smith's tackle during the third Test in Sydney.

A scoreline of 26–12 in Great Britain's favour had not come about by chance nor had it been helped by the departure of Australia's Peter Sterling in the thirty-third minute, suffering from a bruised shoulder. This great win had been achieved by the skills and courageous 'never say die' attitude of thirteen brave players who defied all the odds to dominate Australia in every phase of the game. All seven forwards (Brian Case joining the fray as substitute for Hugh Waddell in the sixty-fourth minute) tackled tirelessly, none better than Mike Gregory and his captain, Ellery Hanley, who topped the tackle count with thirty-four tackles each. The props Hugh Waddell, a revelation in his Ashes Test debut, and Kevin Ward drove deep and hard into the Australian ranks, at times scattering aside Backo, Bella and Vautin. Roy Powell charged away with the ball out of defence whenever there was trouble, and Paul Hulme crowned his debut as hooker with a robust, wholehearted display which belied his tender years. The solidity of the centres, Stephenson and Loughlin, and the quick cutting edge on the outside provided by the trio of Offiah, Gill and Ford was too much for an Australian side totally paralysed by the tactical superiority of their opponents. And it was the half-backs, Andy Gregory and David Hulme, who were the masters on the day. Gregory's jinking runs and, in tandem with the boot of Paul Loughlin, his tactical kicking had the Australians retreating at regular intervals, while the quiet distribution of David Hulme kept the back line flowing. And when, incidentally, did a British stand-off last make thirty-four tackles in a Test match?

Paul Loughlin began the Test series against Australia at full-back before switching to his more accustomed position at centre for the third Test. His long-striding running style was to cause a number of problems for Australian defences.

Australia's coach, Don Furner, though happy to take the series by two Tests to one, showed his respect for this British side when he generously conceded, 'We were beaten by the better side. We gave them too much room to move. We were completely outplayed.' I have never seen an Australian team so stunned and shocked at the close of a game, their stares of disbelief at the thought of anyone daring to beat them will remain forever with me. And I have no doubt that the memory of this great Test match, Britain's first victory for ten years, will remain for ever with Mal Reilly too. His departure from the field, chaired by his loyal players, was a fitting tribute to his perseverance, his energy and his inspiration when, only twenty-four hours before, all had seemed lost.

116

Sadly, only 15,944 spectators were at the Sydney Football Stadium to see one of the greatest Test matches of all time but those who did, especially the British supporters, will no doubt at some distant date in the future stand proud and say, 'I know, because I was there'.

Phil Ford celebrates his outstanding solo try in the third Test in Sydney. Henderson Gill looks on in wonder.

Ellery Hanley, surrounded by cheering fans, after the Lions' great victory in the third Test in Sydney.

Australia: Jack; Ettingshausen, O'Connor, Jackson, Currie; Lewis, Sterling; Bella, Conescu, Backo, Fullerton-Smith, Vautin, Pearce

Substitutes: Belcher for Sterling after 33 minutes, Lindner for Fullerton-Smith after 66 minutes

Scorers: tries – Backo, Lewis; goals – O'Connor (2)

Great Britain: Phil Ford (Bradford Northern); Gill (Wigan), Loughlin (St Helens), Stephenson (Leeds), Offiah (Widnes); David Hulme (Widnes), Andy Gregory (Wigan); Ward (Castleford), Paul Hulme (Widnes), Waddell (Oldham), Powell (Leeds), Mike Gregory (Warrington), Hanley (Wigan)

Substitutes: Case for Waddell after 64 minutes, Wright not used

Scorers: tries – Gill (2), Offiah, Phil Ford, Mike Gregory; goals – Loughlin (3)

Referee: F. Desplas (France)

Attendance: 15,944

Needless to say, the mood of the players on the short journey across the Tasman Sea to New Zealand was a happy one, with a burst of choral singing led by the irrepressible Andy Gregory from the rear of the plane. The stereo-cassette players, out of which comes an endless stream of Funk or Reggae-style music, and which are now standard head-dress for any aspiring League international, were cast aside and the spirit of 'togetherness', of a team which has experienced the worst and battled through, was evident. The elements, too, on arrival in the 'windy city' of Wellington looked favourably on the Lions: three days of glorious winter sunshine greeted the tourists and set the scene for a lively match against the local side, superbly coached by the former Kiwi and Wigan hooker, Howie Tamati. The size of the crowd, 4,680, the largest for about forty years, and the enthusiasm of the team, inspired by James Leuluai, indicated the growing profile of Rugby League in this Union stronghold. Happily for the visitors, though Leuluai led the Wellington charge with two tries to establish an 18–12 lead only thirteen minutes from time, three tries within eight minutes by the fitter and faster Great Britain side, from Karl Fairbank (2) and Andy Currier saw them scrape home by 24–18.

It was a shaky win by the reserve team but on arrival in Christchurch, in preparation for the important World Cup qualifying match against New Zealand at the Addington Showground on the coming Sunday, Mal Reilly was in the happy position of being able to report a clean bill of health. After a light training session on the Thursday afternoon he named Kevin Beardmore, missing from the third Australian Test with a bruised hip, at hooker at the expense of Widnes's Paul Hulme. The Widnes youngster had performed above all expectations when making his Test debut, and though there was some concern that a winning side had to be changed, the coach insisted that he needed his first-choice hooker in the team. 'Paul Hulme did a marvellous job in very difficult circumstances and I was proud of him', Reilly said. 'But we need a specialist hooker for such an important match and Kevin has averaged three strikes against the head in the Tests so far.'

Christchurch, New Zealand may lack the intense Rugby League atmosphere that is almost tangible in Sydney, but as Reilly and his squad worked hard in training on the Friday and Saturday it was not difficult to sense that some special event was to take place in this usually quiet garden city of the South Island. Taxi drivers spoke of clients seeking tickets for the match, shoppers chatted about the Kiwis' chances of success and local punters sought bets on the outcome of a match that was to fill the ground with more spectators than had watched a League game in the province of Canterbury for over sixty years.

Christchurch
17 July
(World Cup
qualifying
match)

New Zealand 12 v Great Britain 10

It was to the credit of the Kiwis that they overcame the driving rain and thick clinging mud of the Addington Showground to win this important World Cup match. But, sad to say, the game will be remembered in years to come as the one in which Great Britain contrived to beat themselves. Facing the blustery wind, the Lions should have taken complete control but instead were led 12–8 at half-time by a Kiwi side which had been presented with only two try-scoring chances and which had accepted both of them gratefully. Loughlin's opening try in the first minute gave Great Britain the start they needed in such vile playing conditions; and the manner of the try indicated that the Kiwi defence was far from impregnable. A sharp break from the scrum saw David Hulme round his man and, though losing the ball in the tackle, Paul Loughlin was in support to snatch the ball to score, after a ricochet from an unlucky Kevin Iro. Loughlin missed the comparatively easy kick against a wind which was eventually to ruin the Lions hopes of a commanding lead. A further try from David Hulme himself, after a well timed pass from Ellery Hanley, again indicated the confidence within the team. However, David Stephenson, succeeding Loughlin as goal-kicker, saw his shot carried beyond the far post by the wind in the manner of Loughlin's previous penalty attempt from in front of the posts. In contrast to these weak attempts at goal the Kiwi prop, Peter Brown, admittedly aided by the wind, had kicked two penalties, both for Great Britain's indiscipline at play-the-balls, to complement the excellent pair of tries by the New Zealand substitute, Gary Freeman.

Stepping on to the pitch in the thirteenth minute for the injured Mark Horo, Freeman's move to stand-off and Shane Cooper's switch to loose forward transformed the Kiwis' play. Following Brown's goal, Gary Freeman edged the Kiwis ahead when, in the sixteenth minute, he ran on to a masterly pass from Shane Cooper, the length and accuracy of which left Stephenson and Hulme stranded. Freeman raced down the left touchline, even offering Phil Ford and Paul Loughlin, Britain's last line of defence, two contemptuous dummies before scoring.

Freeman was on hand again on the stroke of half-time when, with the score evenly balanced at 8–8, he was the last to handle in a five-man movement which swept across the Lions' 25-yard line. The Kiwi second-rower, Sam Stewart, a

119

stalwart in defence in the later stages of the match, proved most effective here in holding himself upright in the tackle near to Great Britain's try-line before giving the final pass to the grateful Freeman.

After the match Britain had every right to bemoan the decision of the Australian referee, Mick Stone, in disallowing what seemed a perfectly good try to Andy Gregory in the twenty-fifth minute by declaring the pass from the man-of-the-match, Kevin Ward, to have been forward. A Lions' try then would probably have won the match but, when Paul Loughlin, now with the wind at his back, pulled back a further two points with a penalty for offside, only three minutes into the second half, there should have been no doubt about a Great Britain win.

That the Lions lost this vital match and failed to qualify for the World Cup final against Australia was caused by a variety of factors. As the weather and the state of the pitch deteriorated in the second half so Britain's handling skills proved more fallible and their ability to open out play to the backs more risky. When Ellery Hanley was forced to leave the field in the sixty-seventh minute with a nasty cut across both lids of his right eye the Lions lost their most gifted player and captain in the most vital quarter of the match. Yet it was with their tactical kicking that Britain really lost their way and allowed the Kiwis to escape with a win.

Paul Loughlin, as well as running boldly and bravely out of defence, at times contained New Zealand near their try-line with punishing long punts down field. But in the final half-hour, with neither side able to score a try from a handling movement and with the ferocious tackling of both sides creating a stalemate, there was a need for an old-fashioned 'up-and-under'. The selection of the experienced hooker, Kevin Beardmore, proved a wise decision as he dominated the second-half scrums by 11–5. Thus, the Lions had an abundant supply of possession, yet never once did they test the Kiwi full-back, Darrell Williams, with any high kicks. In such atrocious conditions and with such a slippery ball he would almost certainly have made the mistakes which could have led to the try Britain needed so desperately. Instead, Andy Gregory, especially, kicked wide and too deep and rarely troubled the Kiwis. Not once did the Lions attempt a drop-goal when, with an ample supply of ball and with the props, Hugh Waddell and Kevin Ward, barnstorming down the middle of the field, plenty of opportunities could have been created and, incidentally, in the most grassed and least sodden part of the pitch.

Great Britain allowed the Kiwis to dictate terms with their keen tackling and were led into a contest of brute strength in midfield when a little thought could have saved much wasted energy. And yet, in a contest of such intensity and played under such trying conditions, it would be churlish to criticise too much the players of either side.

Paul Loughlin used his size and long stride to good effect with powerful runs down the flanks; David Hulme and Andy Gregory tried hard to engineer moves around the scrum; and none did better than Great Britain's front row of Hugh Waddell, Kevin Beardmore, and Kevin Ward. All three tackled strongly, ran the ball with fierce determination and throughout the match provided a possession ratio from the scrum of 2 to 1 heels. But New Zealand had their heroes, too, especially in that final thirty-minute period when they

120

were rarely able to venture out of their own half, such was the possession count against them. Sam Stewart led the defence with an incredible count of forty-one tackles; the hooker, Wayne Wallace, proved lively in the loose; and the combination of Clayton Friend and Gary Freeman, at half-back for all but thirteen minutes' play, troubled Great Britain.

At the final whistle the Great Britain team filed disconsolately from the field, knowing that their tour had come to an end, and a sad one too. The giant Kiwi prop, Adrian Shelford, a tower of strength in the close forward exchanges, left the field with the jersey of the Lions prop, Hugh Waddell, draped round his neck and a huge grin shining out from beneath the mud pack which covered his face. Both sides had given everything, but New Zealand, by luck, by better judgement, and some skill had clung to the vital two points difference that was to give them a place in their first-ever World Cup final.

Great Britain still had to pull on their jerseys once more against Auckland two days later and it was was no surprise that a weary outfit conceded five tries as Auckland ran out worthy winners by 30–14. Only Henderson Gill's two tries raised a flicker of life in the British camp, all their energy sunk beneath the Christchurch mud.

New Zealand: Williams; Shane Horo, Bell, Kevin Iro, Mercer; Cooper, Friend; Brown, Wallace, Shelford, Graham, Stewart, Mark Horo

Substitutes: Freeman for Mark Horo after 13 minutes, Faimolo not used

Scorers: tries – Freeman (2); goals – Brown

Great Britain: Phil Ford (Bradford Northern); Gill (Wigan), Stephenson (Leeds), Loughlin (St Helens), Offiah (Widnes); David Hulme (Widnes), Andy Gregory (Wigan); Ward (Castleford), Beardmore (Castleford), Waddell (Oldham), Mike Gregory (Warrington), Powell (Leeds), Hanley (Wigan)

Substitutes: Paul Hulme for Hanley after 67 minutes, Wright not used

Scorers: tries – Loughlin, David Hulme; goal – Loughlin

Referee: M. Stone (Australia)

Attendance: 8,545

With no fewer than nine members of the original Great Britain party – Des Drummond, Joe Lydon, Steve Hampson, Paul Medley, Shaun Edwards, Garry Schofield, Lee Crooks, Andy Platt and Paul Dixon – either so badly injured during the tour that they had to return home, or for various reasons unable to leave home at all, an objective assessment of the tour and of the comparative playing strengths of Australia, New Zealand and Great Britain is quite exceptionally difficult.

No touring party in Rugby League history, whether Lion or Kangaroo, whether Kiwi or Kumul, has been buffetted by so many blows of ill fortune as this Great Britain squad and no coach could ever afford to lose players of such quality and reputation and be successful. Yet had all those nine been with the party throughout the tour, their presence might well have hidden the weaknesses of our domestic game, which only came to light by the players' absence. And, ironically, their very absence highlighted strengths which the British game must utilise in the future.

The manager, Les Bettinson, indicated that 'in Papua New Guinea we realised that we had only one Test team', and his coach, Mal Reilly, after watching an horrific performance by his team at Orange in New South Wales could only utter, 'What can I say?' Their statements underlined the predicament that they and the assistant coach, Phil Larder, found themselves in when players became unavailable. It is easy, with hindsight, to declare that there were selection mistakes but I do feel that the coaches were given bad advice from people at home with regard to some of the players eventually chosen.

The players created a wonderful team spirit all the time, gave of their best in the training sessions and never shirked a match when called upon to play. But there were many on the tour who were simply out of their depth, even against the country sides. And though the generous Mal Reilly at the end of the tour insisted that 'it has been a pleasure to be associated with the players', he really should not have to start teaching international players the basic skills of the game, nor should it be necessary to raise the fitness levels of an international squad by as much as twenty per cent in order to compete at Test level.

The gap left by the non-available and injured players showed how shallow is the pool of really talented players in Britain and how inadequate are the coaching arrangements at many of our major clubs. Hence the problem confronting Mal Reilly throughout the tour was how to protect his Test players from injury as well as fielding teams that could perform creditably against even moderate opposition. Such were the weaknesses of some of the players that after the disasters at Manly, Tamworth, and Orange the strongest sides available had to be selected, regardless of Test commitments, in order to maintain morale and to continue to promote the tour. It was to Ellery Hanley's credit that the captain urged his selection in as many matches as possible and led everywhere by example.

At least, the horrendous injury problems helped the development of some of the younger players, notably Paul Loughlin who, whether at centre or at full-back in all five Test matches, proved a strong attacking player and a skilled kicker of a ball. The two Hulme brothers, David and Paul, applied themselves vigorously to whatever task they were allotted on the field and, at times, revealed talents that many were unaware they possessed.

Martin Offiah, with nineteen tries on tour, overcame his inexperience at Test level to prove that in the future he will be a most dangerous opponent, while Phil Ford's elusive running and importance as a utility player demonstrated what a valuable tourist he had become. Much responsibility fell upon the shoulders of Andy Gregory and Ellery Hanley and neither were found wanting. Both revealed a full array of skills and in all matches, except perhaps in the second Test against Australia, at Brisbane, dominated the British teams for which they played.

At the end of the tour Les Bettinson considered that, 'Our players here benefitted from knowing that they can hold Australia and New Zealand. No longer will we cave in to a physical battering or from pressure exerted by the pack. Australia should never again run rampant by virtue of superior strength and fitness.' I would agree with his judgement and suggest that with such players as Kevin Ward, Kevin Beardmore and Hugh Waddell, we have an outstandingly successful front row to match that of any other country, and in Mike Gregory a truly world-class second-row forward. Roy Powell, Paul Dixon, and Andy Platt can be considered forwards of equal calibre to the best in Australia and New Zealand.

Britain's lack of playing resources capable of matching the opposition in midweek matches was aggravated by the folly of the itinerary which the tourists had to contend with. No Lions team should have to play Manly or a President's XIII only four days before a Test match in Australia and no longer can the Great Britain management consider sending their side vast distances, at great cost, to places like Gympie in Queensland or playing a combined Brisbane team before pitifully small crowds.

The Australians must cast aside their present parochial attitude which gives precedence to the Sydney Premiership competition over an international tour. They must realise that Great Britain can no longer 'fly the flag' at League outposts at their expense. The Lions, in future, should play the top Australian sides, such as Manly, the Brisbane Broncos, Canberra, and Newcastle Knights at the weekend when large gates can be attracted and, if country districts must be played, then a way of funding the matches must be worked out. It is ludicrous that the proceeds from a single sponsored players' 'golf day' at Manly should raise profits equal to the gate receipts from three country matches. And the business manager on this tour, David Howes, like Roland Davis in 1984, should not be forced to haggle with turnstile operators, check the fencing of a ground for holes through which supporters can creep, and argue with secretaries over the authenticity of declared gate receipts. If the tourists must play at country venues, then a financial guarantee should be fixed in advance. Because of the weaknesses of some of the teams Great Britain have fielded in the past against the country-area sides, or because of the saturation coverage on television of Rugby League in Australia, these visits are not as attractive to the public as they used to be. Incidentally, it is worth noting that, in New Zealand, crowds in the Wellington and Christchurch areas exceeded all expectations and augur well for the financial viability of the 1990 Lions tour of that country.

In 1984, at the end of that year's Lions' tour of Australia and New Zealand, I wrote that I was greatly concerned at the standard of coaching in British clubs. In 1988, and with only one more Test-match win recorded, it might seem that little progress has been made on that front. Not so: for despite the actual playing record of the 1988 Lions, if the continuity of coach and management can be maintained, I believe we are making real progress at last and have laid the foundations for the success of Rugby League at international level.

At times the manager, coaches, and medical staff joked that some malign spirit was dogging their heels and would not relent. That Great Britain could, against all the odds, secure a comprehensive victory over Australia and be only two points adrift of New Zealand in that tense World Cup qualifier, speaks volumes for their application, dedication, and professionalism. I cannot fault them in any respect.

Both Les Bettinson and David Howes went about their duties with an air of calm whatever crises might be current at the time. Les Bettinson handled his players with a gentle discipline to which they responded admirably and David Howes tried every way to bolster revenue for the tour, invariably with promotional flair and success, amid a difficult economic climate in Australia. Nothing was too much trouble for Dr Forbes MacKenzie and the party's physiotherapist, Geoff Plummer. Their 'field hospital', set up in the team's hotel, proved invaluable for the immediate treatment of players returning from a match in the early hours of the morning.

One had only to walk along the corridor of the players' floor to form an idea of the application of Mal Reilly and his assistant, Phil Larder. An array of notices set out every statistical detail from the previous match: tackle counts, mistakes made, team arrangements and training sessions to be held, the type of dress to wear on all occasions and a host of material designed to brief the players as fully as possible.

Phil Larder's work with the videos of matches highlighted the strengths and weaknesses of the opposition and his analysis of players helped the team enormously. The coaching and training sessions of Mal Reilly were most impressive, well constructed, and always varied. It was a credit to him that, under intense pressure at times, he could sustain the intensity of training twice a day and earn the respect of all his players for his devotion to duty. No coach has ever earned a Test win more than Mal Reilly. He fully deserved his manager's tribute. 'Malcolm was a tower of strength. His playing resources at times were so limited yet he never once deviated from his belief that his team could beat Australia.'

The Rugby Football League must now consider changing the present rule that a national coach cannot coach at club level so that Mal Reilly, appointed coach at Leeds in the course of the tour, can be asked to stay on as national coach. And the same management team, too, must surely be considered for future tours. So much important groundwork on fitness and attitude has been accomplished, so much has been learned about the players, and about the process of selection, that there must be an element of continuity if we are to regain our position as world leaders.

The tour also taught us a lot about the game in Britain today. We must inject more professionalism at all levels, from the club chairman to the most junior player. Players, certainly in the major clubs, should be given greater financial incentives to intensify their attitude to rugby, and both players and coaches must think more about each match and its preparation. There must be a unified and truly committed effort from coaches, administrators and players, and coaches like Mal Reilly and Phil Larder must be listened to at the expense of those who scoff at anything which smacks of an informed and intelligent approach to coaching.

Britain did not win the Ashes, and they failed to qualify for the World Cup final, but progress will have been achieved if those willing to learn and impart new coaching techniques and improved standards of fitness are allowed to have their say. Mal Reilly declared that his team had 'overcome a mental barrier in defeating Australia'. 'They are not supermen,' he said, 'and British players should now be able to consider themselves as their equals.'

Whatever the players thought at the end of their tour, I know that the experience of that historic third Test victory at Sydney will live with me for ever. I will remember the joy on the faces of the British players and the relief on Mal Reilly's as confirmation that dedication and hard work do find their rewards, eventually.

A Summary of the Tour

22 May v Papua New Guinea (World Cup qualifying match). Great Britain won 42–22

Papua New Guinea: tries – Kovae (2), Krewanty, Rop;
goals – Numapo (3)

Great Britain: tries – Schofield (2), Gill (2), Medley, Mike Gregory, Stephenson; goals – Loughlin (7)

Referee: G McCallum (Australia)

Attendance: 12,000

24 May v District XIII. Great Britain won 36–18

Great Britain: tries – Offiah (3), Phil Ford (2), Schofield; goals – Crooks (5), Schofield

Attendance: 4,000

27 May v North Queensland. Great Britain won 66–16

Great Britain: tries – Offiah (4), Mike Ford (3), Medley (2), Phil Ford (2), Dixon; goals – Stephenson (8), Phil Ford

Referee: B Gomersall

Attendance: 8,000

1 June v Newcastle Knights. Great Britain won 28–12

Great Britain: tries – Ward, Offiah (2), Hanley (2); goals – Loughlin (4)

Referee: G McCallum

Attendance: 7,700

5 June v Northern Division. Great Britain lost 12–36

   Great Britain: tries – Gill, Schofield; goals – Loughlin (2)

   Referee: B Priest

   Attendance: 2,000

7 June v Manly. Great Britain lost 0–30

   Referee: F Desplas

   Attendance: 11,131

11 June v Australia (First Test). Great Britain lost 6–17

   Australia: tries – Backo, Jackson (2); goals – O'Connor (2); drop-goal – Lewis

   Great Britain: try – Hanley; goal – Loughlin

   Referee: F Desplas

   Attendance: 24,480

15 June v Combined Brisbane XIII. Great Britain won 28–14

   Great Britain: tries – Offiah (2), Schofield, Fairbank, Mike Ford; goals – Stephenson (4)

   Referee: D Manson

   Attendance: 1,825

17 June v Central Queensland. Great Britain won 64–8

   Great Britain: tries – Offiah (3), Fairbank (3), Hanley (2), Gibson (2), Powell; goals – Loughlin (10)

   Referee: L Crane

   Attendance: 5,000

22 June v Toowoomba. Great Britain won 28–12

   Great Britain: tries – Hanley (2), Mike Gregory (2), Phil Ford; goals – Loughlin (4)

   Referee: T Bliss

   Attendance: 4,000

25 June v Wide Bay. Great Britain won 14–0

Great Britain: tries – Currier, Offiah, Phil Ford; goal – Loughlin

Referee: R Leis

Attendance: 2,210

28 June v Australia (Second Test). Great Britain lost 14–34

Australia: tries – O'Connor, Jackson, Ettingshausen, Backo, Lewis, Pearce; goals – O'Connor (5)

Great Britain: tries – Phil Ford, Offiah; goals – Loughlin (3)

Referee: F Desplas

Attendance: 27,130

3 July v Western Division. Great Britain won 28–26

Great Britain: tries – Groves, Hanley, Offiah (2), Currier; goals – Currier (4)

Referee: P Robinson (replaced by P Ryan after 51 minutes)

Attendance: 3,506

5 July v President's XIII. Great Britain lost 16–24

Great Britain: tries – Phil Ford (2), Mike Gregory; goals – Loughlin (2)

Referee: E Ward

Attendance: 6,037

9 July v Australia (Third Test and World Cup qualifying match). Great Britain won 26–12

Australia: tries – Backo, Lewis; goals – O'Connor (2)

Great Britain: tries – Gill (2), Offiah, Phil Ford, Mike Gregory; goals – Loughlin (3)

Referee: F Desplas

Attendance: 15,994

13 July v Wellington. Great Britain won 24–18

Great Britain: tries – Fairbank (2), Currier, Eyres; goals – Currier, Stephenson, Loughlin (2)

Referee: D Sullivan

Attendance: 4,680

17 July v New Zealand (World Cup qualifying match). Great Britain lost 10–12

New Zealand: tries – Freeman (2); goals – Brown (2)

Great Britain: tries – Loughlin, David Hulme; goals – Loughlin

Referee: M Stone (Australia)

Attendance: 8,545

19 July v Auckland. Great Britain lost 14–30

Great Britain: tries – Gill (2); goals – Loughlin (3)

Referee: P Shrimpton

Attendance: 10,000

Players' Tour Record

Player	P	S★	Trs	Gls	Pts
Beadmore (Castleford)	9	0	0	0	0
Case (Wigan)	7	1	0	0	0
Currier (Widnes)	5	0	3	5	22
Crooks (Leeds)	3	2	0	5	10
Dixon (Halifax)	6	2	1	0	4
Edwards (Wigan)	1	0	0	0	0
Eyres (Widnes)	3	0	1	0	4
Fairbank (Bradford N)	9	1	6	0	24
Michael Ford (Oldham)	7	0	5	0	20
Phil Ford (Bradford N)	13	0	9	1	38
Gibson (Leeds)	9	1	2	0	8
Gill (Wigan)	10	2	7	0	28
Andy Gregory (Wigan)	8	0	0	0	0
Mike Gregory (Warrington)	10	0	5	0	20
Groves (St Helens)	8	0	1	0	4
Haggerty (St Helens)	5	2	0	0	0
Hanley (Wigan)	10	1	8	0	32
David Hulme (Widnes)	11	2	1	0	4
Paul Hulme (Widnes)	4	3	0	0	0
Joyner (Castleford)	3	0	0	0	0
Loughlin (St Helens)	11	2	1	43	90
Medley (Leeds)	5	0	3	0	12
Offiah (Widnes)	11	2	19	0	76
Platt (St Helens)	5	0	0	0	0
Powell (Leeds)	12	2	1	0	4
Schofield (Leeds)	5	0	5	1	22
Stephenson (Leeds)	11	0	1	13	30
Waddell (Oldham)	10	3	0	0	0
Ward (Castleford)	10	0	1	0	4
Wilkinson (Halifax)	6	0	0	0	0
Wright (Widnes)	7	1	0	0	0

S★ = appearance as a substitute.

3

Looking Ahead 1988–89

A Preview of the Season, the Fixtures, and a Directory of the Clubs

Scott Gale was one of many Australians who signed for British clubs during the 1987–88 season. Whether Hull would have been spared their worries in the championship had this strong and skilful half-back or centre not been so seriously injured in his first match that he had to go back to Australia is anyone's guess. Certainly his return for Hull's two semi-finals in the Challenge Cup helped to lift the team during their astonishing revival in the last weeks of the season.

Looking Ahead 1988–89
A Preview of the Season

Harry Edgar

One could start this preview, almost automatically, with the cliché, 'the new season will be one of challenge.' Instead, let me quote the late Eddie Waring, writing his preview of a new season forty years ago. Eddie, quite probably the best publicist Rugby League has ever had, and an inspiring campaigning journalist in his pre-television days, summed up the rapidly approaching 1948–49 season, thus:

> Rugby League football is still not a national game and the only people who love it are Rugby League folk themselves. Small-mindedness, petty jealousies, false pride and envy, has retarded the progress of the game long enough. Despite everything, the game has survived and prospered simply because it is such a good game. Every single person who likes the code can do it some good and assist in its future, which I still believe could be a national one. Do we continue to crawl or can we really stride out this season? I wonder.'

As Eddie Waring wondered back in 1948, I wonder again in 1988. Perhaps it is a sentiment that could have been expressed at the dawn of every new season since the game's birth in 1895, as few sports face such challenges as Rugby League because few have such vast potential for growth still untapped. However, though it has been a long time coming, there are signs now that 1988–89 might just be the watershed season for Rugby League in Britain.

Sadly, we won't now have the immediate attraction of a World Cup final in this country in the early weeks of the season. Against New Zealand on 17 July Great Britain finished just two points away from the result that would have given us the chance to host the final against Australia. As Britain's hopes of victory slithered away in the Christchurch mud, so did visions of another 50,000 crowd at Old Trafford, Manchester and a marvellous promotional opportunity for the game in the United Kingdom. Instead it is the Kiwis who look forward to staging the World Cup final, and, in doing so, will be able to take further giant strides forward for Rugby League in their country. And, after their efforts during the past three or four years, few would deny that the New Zealand League deserves that opportunity.

For British Rugby League it is now a question of accepting the challenge of expansion and development of a sport still extremely restricted in this country, both geographically and socially. First, we must recognise the importance of student Rugby League in throwing off the shackles in both categories. But now there is to be a new streamlined executive controlling the Rugby Football League; the establishment of the Rugby League Foundation with a view to

The Australian
Test star, Dale
Shearer, played
impressively for
Widnes in the
middle of the
1987–88 season
and helped them
overcome the
loss of the
injured Tony
Myler.

providing financial support for those involved in developing and improving the game; and acceptance on all sides that the professional game must work in harmony with BARLA for the promotion of youth rugby and for the betterment of the game as a whole.

The recently appointed national development officer, Tom O'Donovan, sets out on his first full season to help Rugby League put down roots in areas outside the traditional centres of Lancashire, Yorkshire and Cumbria. In those so-called 'traditional' areas, a network of local amateur league development officers is steadily being built up, with support from local authorities giving the game a privileged position within the community of many northern towns and cities.

These are the signs that give me confidence that 1988–89 will be the season in which British Rugby League actively starts building the firm foundations of the pyramid that will lead, ultimately, to widespread excellence and prosperity. The groundwork has been done, now the real moves forward, fashioned with care and imagination, can begin.

It has to be that way. There can be no short cuts. On the surface, Rugby League at the top level in Britain is on a high. A crowd boom saw attendances rise by over 20% in the first division last season; Wembley was a massive sell-out; and the leading clubs regularly provided scintillating entertainment on the field of play. There are no reasons to suppose that this will not continue. What is obvious, however, is that the clubs whose fans have spent the summer waiting for the new season with the greatest excitement, are those which are expecting to sign major overseas players. The impact of Australian and New Zealand players on British clubs over the past three or four years has been enormous, and a major factor in the resurgence of public interest in Rugby League.

This year's crop of imported stars promises to be as good as ever, with St Helens leading the way, having recruited the brilliant Michael O'Connor as well as the returning Knowsley Road hero of last season, Shane Cooper. Wakefield Trinity, making a bold, and seemingly well-financed, bid for a return to the élite, have the former Kiwi captain, Mark Graham, on the way to a two-year contract, while Trinity's near neighbours, Castleford, will have one of Australia's most talked about and controversial footballers, Ron Gibbs, wearing their amber and black colours in 1988–89.

Warrington should have an awesome pack with the powerful Australian duo, Steve Roach and Les Davidson, along with the mercurial Phil Blake in the backs, and Leeds supporters eagerly await the return of the dashing Andrew Ettingshausen who provided so much flair and spectacular entertainment at Headingley two seasons ago. Numerous other highly rated players from 'down under' will be arriving early in the season to don the colours of British clubs, thus guaranteeing increased public interest wherever they play.

I don't subscribe to the view that overseas players have restricted the emergence of home-grown stars. Young potential talent is around and, to date, its greatest ally in many professional clubs has been the very presence of those outstanding Australian and New Zealand players, giving advice, encouraging positive attitudes to playing and training, and generally helping to produce the self-discipline, skills and tactics which, though some less enlightened British

Eric Fitzsimons, one of the game's outstanding
young coaches, did well to take Oldham not
only back to the first division at the first
attempt at the end of the 1987–88 season but
also to win the second division Premiership
Trophy after an enthralling game against
Featherstone Rovers.

coaches still seem unable to accept the fact, help to produce successful Rugby League teams.

It has been the inadequacies of some of those involved in the game off the field that has proved most damaging. Those officials who have been content to sign overseas stars on short-term contracts, while paying little attention to the development of junior sides in their own areas, have simply taken advantage of the excellence of Australian Rugby League's coaching and development policy. They have, to date, shown little understanding of how the production line of antipodean League talent has come about, and little inclination to create their own system of improving standards to a comparable level.

Moreover, they have shown little respect for the Rugby League's own admirable National Coaching Scheme, which is now producing new young coaches of high calibre, though as yet unable to play active rôles in many professional clubs because some officials still fall into the trap of preferring former well-known 'name' players, regardless of their capabilities as coaches.

Some British club officials have been content to jet off to Australia during recent summers, carrying open cheque-books, apparently determined to sign up their full quota of Australian players, come what may. Yet many come home blissfully unaware of the extent to which the Australian Rugby League has created an environment that encourages talented young people to dedicate themselves to League. However, while the 1988–89 season will see another crop of well known Australasian players adding welcome skills and crowd-pulling charisma to the leading British clubs, it is at last being realised that what is needed to improve standards are long-term strategies for developing and coaching local talent.

With that in mind, the trend towards importing coaches looks set to begin in earnest this season, as clubs look further afield for mentors with the skills to bring the best out of their players (and soon, one would like to think, to work in harness with the young graduates from the National Coaching Scheme). The remarkable successes of Chris Anderson at Halifax and Graham Lowe at Wigan support the argument for bringing in overseas coaches. Both Hull and Castleford have been brave enough to opt for new blood in 1988–89 with their decisions to employ two of the Australian League's most able young coaching talents, Brian Smith and Darryl Van de Velde.

The antipodean coaching flavour will be continued by Rod Reddy, starting his second season with Barrow, and, of course, at Halifax, where the Queenslander, Ross Strudwick, joins forces with Graham Eadie – and takes over where Chris Anderson left off, certainly a hard act to follow.

The first division championship and major cup competitions look set to be more intense than ever before, as more and more clubs work hard to improve their standards, confident that success on the field will attract the big crowds necessary to cover the additional financial outlay of signing new players. It was Wigan who set such impressive standards in their championship season two years ago, and now neighbours St Helens, Widnes and Warrington have shown themselves capable of matching their Central Park rivals. Leeds, with the coup of recruiting the Great Britain coach, Malcolm Reilly, will be eager to continue the momentum that saw average attendances at Headingley last season rise by over 3,000 per game. Much attention will be focussed on the two Hull clubs:

only a few years ago Humberside was deemed the capital city of British Rugby League, but more recent performances and public support have slipped disturbingly. Stringent efforts will be made in 1988–89 to see the 'sleeping giants' of the east coast awake.

A fourteen-club first division is sure to be extremely competitive, with little margin for error. We can expect a stronger than usual challenge from the three newly promoted teams this season, with both Oldham and Wakefield Trinity willing and able to speculate large amounts of money on recruiting the type of players they believe will help them to re-live former glories. Featherstone Rovers, meanwhile, do not have the same financial resources, neither would the mantle of signing stars fit comfortably with this champion of the little clubs. What Featherstone do have is one of Britain's most positive and charismatic coaches in Peter Fox, a man quite capable of moulding successful teams without big money signings.

So, there is little doubt that another exciting and rewarding season is ahead in Britain. The rules of the modern game make Rugby League more open and spectacular than it has ever been. The Australian influence on the British game, which has been apparent since the 1982 Kangaroo tour delivered such a shock to the system (and which coincided with the launch of Phil Larder's National Coaching Scheme), has forced us to improve standards. The results are there for all to see, with steadily growing attendances, sponsorship support and respect.

All this optimism, however, is only half the story. There are another twenty clubs in the second division, and here lie the major challenges for the game's administrators as the gap between the two divisions widens. While talk of a super league may be justified in terms of providing the high levels of intense weekly competition needed if Britain's players are going to to be able to meet Australia in Test matches on consistently equal terms, the League cannot just abandon its other twenty member clubs to a lifetime of being second best.

Many of those clubs are situated in traditional areas of Rugby League where the amateur game is strong and public interest well established and waiting for an incentive to be enticed back into active support. The present structure of the game, with the rich getting more powerful and the poor perhaps slipping further back, does not provide much incentive for potential supporters to return in large numbers to the second-division clubs, apart from the occasional cup run when they have the chance to play top-class opposition. None of the struggling second-division clubs must be allowed to become a brake on the overall development and promotion of the game. At the same time, the Rugby Football League, with responsibilities to the sport as a whole, must not throw all its eggs into the basket containing the dozen or so Lancashire and Yorkshire-based clubs who happen to be on top at the moment.

My own view is that any super league should be one of professionally administered clubs situated in areas designated by the League's governing body. That would mean, in some traditional areas, some teams amalgamating to form clubs such as 'Manchester' and 'Cumbria,' as well as high level attempts to establish, and seriously promote, super-league clubs in major cities like London or Cardiff.

Of course this kind of thing is most unlikely to happen in the short term.

136

At the end of the 1987–88 season Chris Anderson returned to Australia after some memorable seasons with Halifax, first as player-coach and then as coach. He will be succeeded as coach by the Australian international Graham Eadie, who will share management duties with another Australian, Ross Strudwick.

Instead, the professional clubs will be left to make the best of the present system, even though for many that means a constant battle for financial survival, with little room for actively promoting and improving the sport in their areas. At the very least, a split into three divisions would seem to be the ideal way of helping to create more incentives for more clubs, and of cutting down the overcrowded fixture-lists that are the achilles heel of British Rugby League, both professional and amateur. A two-division system that sees the same clubs going up and down like a yo-yo, with promoted clubs finding it almost impossible to establish themselves in the top flight, clearly is not working.

For many clubs the problems of the ground safety laws remain a massive burden. Famous old stadiums such as those at Huddersfield, Batley, Dewsbury and Keighley were sad sights last season, and it is hard to imagine there being light at the end of that tunnel in the foreseeable future. There is also likely to be more discussion about clubs changing stadiums during the 1988–89 season. There is still uncertainty surrounding some clubs' plans, but the campaign will start with at least one new name and base, Chorley, the successor to Springfield Borough, which was formed only twelve months before from the remnants of the much-loved Blackpool Borough, as well as three new venues in the second division.

Both Carlisle and Mansfield have plans for new grounds of their own after coming into Rugby League originally as tenants of Football League clubs. For the moment, Mansfield's plans for their own home have been put on ice following the closure of the local colliery, alongside which their new complex was to have been developed; meanwhile Marksman have moved from Alfreton in Derbyshire back to Nottinghamshire, to share facilities with Sutton Town, the Northern Premier League soccer club, for the duration of the 1988–89 season. At least Sutton is in the same county as Mansfield! Rochdale Hornets are planning to vacate the Athletic Grounds, once a venue for cup finals and Test matches, to enter a ground-sharing arrangement with the local soccer club at Spotland. Both York and Hull Kingston Rovers are likely to make the 1988–89 season the last at their traditional homes, before selling to real estate developers and moving to newly constructed stadiums twelve months hence. I shall particularly miss York's Clarence Street ground, one of the most picturesque in the League, standing as it does in the shadow of the Minster.

From the heady days of the early 1980s, when Fulham pioneered an expansionist boom, the remnants of the League's new clubs have settled down to fight a steady battle for survival rather than be promoted as flagships for the sport's quest to establish itself in new areas. Mansfield and Sheffield struggle along in their own quiet way, surviving on gates of only a few hundred. Yet both will be looking to continue the admirable improvement in playing standards they achieved last season. Carlisle and Fulham have much in common as they keep the League flag flying at opposite ends of the country. Both are given their momentum by a band of tremendously enthusiastic and loyal supporters.

In contrast to the professional League, the amateur game looks set to provide continued enthusiasm for expansion to new areas in the 1988–89 season. In the past, development outside Lancashire, Yorkshire and Cumbria has been purely the result of the efforts of dedicated enthusiasts. Now that the

Andy Goodway survives a tackle from behind
and prepares to pass out in the Wigan v Manly
match in October 1987. Goodway was an
obvious selection for the Lions' tour of
Australasia, and his absence from the party,
for business reasons, was a serious blow for
Great Britain.

The huge success of the Wigan – Manly game
has now given birth to an official World Club
Championship to start this season. Widnes will
play Le Pontet, last season's French
champions, and the winner of that game will
play, in Tokyo, the winner of a southern
hemisphere Australia – New Zealand Club
Challenge.

The mainspring of Featherstone Rovers promotion-winning side in 1987–88 was their scrum-half, Deryck Fox, who organised magnificently a team that grew in confidence as the season wore on. Coached by Peter Fox, one of Britain's most positive and charismatic coaches, Featherstone hope to make a secure place for themselves in the first division during 1988–89.

game has a full-time national development officer, those enthusiasts have someone to turn to for help and guidance. The amateur game's target in the new season must be to come to terms with its over-crowded fixture-lists, and to encourage the development of more clubs with genuine roots, as, for example, Hemel Hempstead have done so successfully, rather than merely rely on transient pub teams to swell the figures of the lists of new amateur clubs.

The National Amateur League begins its third season, committed to taking on board a second division of another ten teams in 1989–90. It may be that we have to wait a while longer before the National League can find worthy entrants from outside the traditional areas, but that must be the eventual aim of the League if the 'N' in NARL is to stand for 'National' and not merely 'Northern' in the eyes of the public. In the short term, the National Amateur League can continue to be strategically placed geographically to ensure that all the traditional strongholds of the game are represented, rather than simply bestowing membership on the first ten clubs who happen to fulfil the basic conditions. In this way, BARLA can continue to set an example for the professional League. It may be that, eventually, the National Amateur League will develop into that third level of competition for the game as a whole – providing a respectable refuge (rather than extinction) for former professional clubs unable to continue the financial struggle, but with supporters who prefer not to give up their traditions or their source of weekend sporting entertainment. And it may also be a place for up-and-coming clubs in new areas to build their strength and the game's presence by promoting a good level of competition. Meanwhile, the National Amateur League has brought new standards of discipline and presentation to the amateur game, and should continue to do only good in 1988–89, with several clubs planning ground and facility improvements.

Challenges abound in other areas of amateur Rugby League. Most significant for the future welfare of the sport as a whole, the 1988–89 season will see the establishment of numerous regional centres of excellence for young players. Part of the new spirit of co-operation between the sport's two governing bodies, in the aftermath of the damaging 'Colts affair,' will be the creation of a new mid-week youth inter-district league, sponsored by British Coal. Each professional club will, in theory, be responsible for helping the development of youth Rugby League in their own area – and the culmination of this first season will be the BARLA Youth tour to Australia in the summer of 1989. The Young Lions, the best amateur Under-19 players in Britain, will be hosted by the Australian High Schools, and any visit to Australia for players of this age should prove educational and instructive.

The summer of 1989 will also see Britain host the second Student World Cup tournament, the first having been won by New Zealand on home soil two years ago. This tournament is an excellent way of encouraging countries to take up the game for the first time to say nothing of the impetus it will provide for student Rugby League within the United Kingdom.

Student involvement brings much fresh talent and a well of enthusiasm to the game. It is most important that the sport's governing bodies recognise this and provide the students' voluntary organisers with the tools required to make the tournament a resounding success. That support will also be needed quickly to maintain the footholds gained so encouragingly by both the Welsh and Scottish students last season.

At the top level of international competition, the 1988–89 season will be less demanding than of late for Great Britain. There are no major tours this season, so the Lions can regroup after their arduous antipodean journey, before facing the annual challenge against France early in the new year. However, Britain does have one prior engagement, when they meet the challenge of a Rest of the World XIII at the end of October, in a celebration match to mark the opening of the game's new Hall of Fame.

Following Britain's emotional success in the third Test in Sydney, the Rest of the World challenge match has been given added impetus. It will be a chance for the British boys to test themselves again against leading Australian and Kiwi opponents and, for the British fans, perhaps a last chance to see such great players as Wally Lewis, Peter Sterling and Wayne Pearce in action. Lewis has said that he will retire from international competition after the World Cup final, though I suspect he may reconsider yet again if Queensland's Wayne Bennett were to be made the next Australian Test coach.

A Continental flavour will be added to the early part of the British season when the French national team, eager to gain as much international experience as possible, will make a mini-tour of the north of England, playing Cumbria plus two club sides, Warrington and Halifax. More Anglo-French interest will be created in the spring when the league champions, Widnes, meet their French counterparts, Le Pontet, home and away, to decide the European club champions, ready to go forward to the world club championship decider against the southern hemisphere nominees. This eventual showdown will be staged as a major televised event in Tokyo, probably in May 1989, and will be Rugby League's first venture into Japan.

In other international developments, the Pacific Cup tournament will be played in Western Samoa during October, with the New Zealand Maoris likely to face a strong challenge for their title this year from both Papua New Guinea and the host nation, who will, incidentally, be coached by the former Kiwi Test captain, Fred Ah Kuoi.

In June 1989 hopes are high that two British clubs, Wigan and Warrington, will play the exhibition game in Milwaukee, Wisconsin, that will, at last, launch the United States Rugby League project on the field of play. There is little doubt that the qualities the Americans would bring to Rugby League would have a major impact on the game world-wide, and specifically in Britain, for over 40% of the USRL is owned by British-based shareholders.

Whether it be from Milwaukee to Mansfield, Sydney to Sheffield, or Western Samoa to Warrington, the spirit of Rugby League remains the same as a new season unfolds. The optimism and enthusiasm are there, among the smell of the linament and the clattering of studs on dressing-room floors throughout the world. 1988–89 will indeed be a season of challenge – and, as my old friend Eddie commented, 'Can we really stride out this season?'. Let us hope so.

The Rugby Football League
Principal Dates, 1988–89

1988	21 August	Okells Charity Shield: Widnes v. Wigan (on the Isle of Man)
	28 August	League season begins
	18 September	County Cup competitions (1st round)
	21 September	Rodstock War of the Roses: Yorkshire v. Lancashire County of Origin (at Headingley, Leeds)
	28 September	County Cup competitions (2nd round)
	5 October	County Cup competitions (semi-finals)
	16 October	John Smith's Yorkshire Cup final
	19 October	Cumbria v. France
	23 October	Grünhalle Lager Lancashire Cup final
	29 October	Whitbread Trophy 'Hall of Fame' celebration: Great Britain v. Rest of the World (at Headingley, Leeds)
	2 November	British Coal Nine-a-side Tournament (at Central Park, Wigan)
	13 November	John Player Special Trophy (1st round)
	27 November	John Player Special Trophy (2nd round)
	4 December	John Player Special Trophy (3rd round)
	10 December	John Player Special Trophy (semi-final 1)
	17 December	John Player Special Trophy (semi-final 2)
1989	7 January	John Player Special Trophy final
	20 January	Great Britain U-20s v. France
	21 January	Whitbread Trophy Test: Great Britain v. France
	29 January	Silk Cut Challenge Cup (1st round)
	4 February	France v. Great Britain U-20s
	5 February	Whitbread Trophy Test: France v. Great Britain (at Avignon)
	12 February	Silk Cut Challenge Cup (2nd round)
	26 February	Silk Cut Challenge Cup (3rd round)
	1 March	World Club Championship: Le Pontet v. Widnes (at Le Pontet)
	11 March	Silk Cut Challenge Cup (semi-final 1)
	15 March	World Club Championship: Widnes v. Le Pontet (at Widnes)
	25 March	Silk Cut Challenge Cup (semi-final 2)
	23 April	Stones Bitter Premiership (1st round)
	29 April	Silk Cut Challenge Cup final (at Wembley Stadium)
	7 May	Stones Bitter Premiership (semi-finals)
	14 May	Stones Bitter Premiership final (at Old Trafford, Manchester)

143

The Rugby Football League Fixtures 1988–89

First Division Fixtures

1988
Sunday 28 August

Featherstone R.	v.	Leeds
Halifax	v.	Widnes
Hull	v.	Castleford
St Helens	v.	Bradford N.
Salford	v.	Hull KR.
Wakefield T.	v.	Warrington
Wigan	v.	Oldham

Sunday 4 September

Bradford N.	v.	Salford
Castleford	v.	Halifax
Hull KR.	v.	Featherstone R.
Oldham	v.	Leeds
Wakefield T.	v.	Wigan
Warrington	v.	St Helens
Widnes	v.	Hull

Sunday 11 September

Featherstone R.	v.	Oldham
Halifax	v.	Bradford N.
Hull	v.	Wakefield T.
Leeds	v.	Widnes
St Helens	v.	Castleford
Salford	v.	Warrington
Wigan	v.	Hull KR.

Sunday 25 September

Bradford N.	v.	Wigan
Castleford	v.	Oldham
Hull KR.	v.	Halifax
Leeds	v.	St Helens
Wakefield T.	v.	Salford
Warrington	v.	Hull
Widnes	v.	Featherstone R.

Sunday 2 October

Featherstone R.	v.	Bradford N.
Halifax	v.	Warrington
Hull	v.	Leeds
Oldham	v.	Hull KR.
St Helens	v.	Wakefield T.
Salford	v.	Widnes
Wigan	v.	Castleford

Sunday 9 October

Bradford N.	v.	Hull
Castleford	v.	Salford
Hull KR.	v.	St Helens
Leeds	v.	Wigan
Wakefield T.	v.	Oldham
Warrington	v.	Featherstone R.
Widnes	v.	Halifax

Sunday 16 October

Featherstone R.	v.	Halifax
Hull KR.	v.	Bradford N.
St Helens	v.	Hull
Salford	v.	Leeds
Widnes	v.	Castleford
Wigan	v.	Wakefield
Warrington	v.	FRANCE

Sunday 23 October

Castleford	v.	Warrington
Hull	v.	Wigan
Leeds	v.	Hull KR.
Oldham	v.	St Helens
Salford	v.	Featherstone R.
Wakefield T.	v.	Widnes
Halifax	v.	FRANCE

Sunday 6 November

Bradford N.	v.	Leeds
Featherstone R.	v.	Castleford
Halifax	v.	Hull
Hull KR.	v.	Wakefield T.
St Helens	v.	Salford
Warrington	v.	Oldham
Wigan	v.	Widnes

Sunday 20 November

Castleford	v.	St Helens
Hull	v.	Featherstone R.
Leeds	v.	Warrington
Oldham	v.	Halifax
Salford	v.	Wigan
Wakefield T.	v.	Bradford N.
Widnes	v.	Hull KR.

Sunday 4 December

Bradford N.	v.	Oldham
Featherstone R.	v.	Salford
Hull KR.	v.	Leeds
St Helens	v.	Halifax
Warrington	v.	Castleford
Widnes	v.	Wakefield T.
Wigan	v.	Hull

Sunday 11 December

Castleford	v.	Widnes
Halifax	v.	Wigan
Hull	v.	St Helens
Leeds	v.	Featherstone R.
Oldham	v.	Warrington
Salford	v.	Bradford N.
Wakefield	v.	Hull KR.

Sunday 18 December

Bradford N.	v.	Castleford
Hull	v.	Oldham
Widnes	v.	Leeds

Monday	Castleford	v.	Hull KR.
26 December	Featherstone R.	v.	Wakefield T.
Boxing Day	Leeds	v.	Halifax
	Oldham	v.	Salford
	St Helens	v.	Wigan
	Warrington	v.	Widnes

1989	Castleford	v.	Bradford N.
Sunday	Leeds	v.	Oldham
1 January	Wakefield T.	v.	Featherstone R.
New Year's Day	Widnes	v.	St Helens
	Wigan	v.	Warrington

Monday			
2 January	Hull KR.	v.	Hull

Sunday	Featherstone R.	v.	Wigan
8 January	Halifax	v.	Castleford
	Hull	v.	Bradford N.
	Oldham	v.	Widnes
	St Helens	v.	Leeds
	Salford	v.	Wakefield T.
	Warrington	v.	Hull KR.

Sunday	Bradford N.	v.	Warrington
15 January	Featherstone R.	v.	St Helens
	Hull KR.	v.	Oldham
	Wakefield T.	v.	Hull
	Widnes	v.	Salford
	Wigan	v.	Halifax

Sunday	Castleford	v.	Wakefield T.
22 January	Halifax	v.	Featherstone R.
	Hull	v.	Widnes
	Leeds	v.	Salford
	Oldham	v.	Bradford N.
	St Helens	v.	Hull KR.
	Warrington	v.	Wigan

Sunday	Bradford N.	v.	Halifax
5 February	Hull KR.	v.	Warrington
	Salford	v.	Hull
	Wakefield T.	v.	Leeds
	Widnes	v.	Oldham

Friday			
17 February	Salford	v.	Castleford

Sunday	Bradford N.	v.	St Helens
19 February	Featherstone R.	v.	Widnes
	Halifax	v.	Hull KR.
	Oldham	v.	Hull
	Wigan	v.	Leeds
	Warrington	v.	Wakefield T.

Sunday	Hull	v.	Halifax
26 February	St Helens	v.	Oldham
	Wakefield T.	v.	Castleford
	Wigan	v.	Featherstone R.

Sunday	Castleford	v.	Hull
5 March	Halifax	v.	Salford
	Hull KR.	v.	Wigan
	Leeds	v.	Wakefield T.
	Oldham	v.	Featherstone R.
	Warrington	v.	Bradford N.

Sunday	Featherstone R.	v.	Hull KR.
12 March	Halifax	v.	Oldham
	Hull	v.	Warrington
	Salford	v.	St Helens
	Wigan	v.	Bradford N.

Sunday	Bradford N.	v.	Widnes
19 March	Hull KR.	v.	Salford
	Leeds	v.	Castleford
	Oldham	v.	Wakefield T.
	St Helens	v.	Featherstone R.
	Warrington	v.	Halifax

Friday	Castleford	v.	Featherstone R.
24 March	Hull	v.	Hull KR.
Good Friday	Leeds	v.	Bradford N.
	Salford	v.	Oldham
	Wakefield T.	v.	Halifax
	Widnes	v.	Warrington
	Wigan	v.	St Helens

Monday	Featherstone R.	v.	Hull
27 March	Halifax	v.	Leeds
Easter Monday	Hull KR.	v.	Castleford
	Oldham	v.	Wigan
	St Helens	v.	Widnes
	Warrington	v.	Salford

Tuesday			
28 March	Bradford N.	v.	Wakefield T.

Sunday	Castleford	v.	Wigan
2 April	Salford	v.	Halifax
	Wakefield T.	v.	St Helens
	Warrington	v.	Leeds
	Widnes	v.	Bradford N.

Sunday	Bradford N.	v.	Featherstone R.
9 April	Halifax	v.	Wakefield T.
	Hull KR.	v.	Widnes
	Leeds	v.	Hull
	Oldham	v.	Castleford
	St Helens	v.	Warrington
	Wigan	v.	Salford

Sunday	Bradford N.	v.	Hull KR.
16 April	Castleford	v.	Leeds
	Featherstone R.	v.	Warrington
	Halifax	v.	St Helens
	Hull	v.	Salford
	Widnes	v.	Wigan

Second Division Fixtures

1988

Friday 26 August	York	v.	Batley

Sunday 28 August	Dewsbury	v.	Runcorn H.
	Doncaster	v.	Fulham
	Hunslet	v.	Chorley B.
	Keighley	v.	Whitehaven
	Mansfield M.	v.	Huddersfield
	Rochdale H.	v.	Barrow
	Sheffield E.	v.	Bramley
	Swinton	v.	Carlisle
	Workington T.	v.	Leigh

Sunday 4 September	Barrow	v.	Mansfield M.
	Bramley	v.	Doncaster
	Carlisle	v.	Batley
	Chorley B.	v.	Workington T.
	Fulham	v.	Sheffield E.
	Huddersfield	v.	Rochdale H.
	Hunslet	v.	Swinton
	Leigh	v.	Runcorn H.
	Whitehaven	v.	Dewsbury
	York	v.	Keighley

Wednesday 7 September	Bramley	v.	Huddersfield
	Keighley	v.	Chorley B.

Sunday 11 September	Dewsbury	v.	Hunslet
	Doncaster	v.	York
	Huddersfield	v.	Fulham
	Keighley	v.	Leigh
	Mansfield M.	v.	Bramley
	Rochdale H.	v.	Whitehaven
	Runcorn H.	v.	Batley
	Sheffield E.	v.	Barrow
	Swinton	v.	Chorley B.
	Workington T.	v.	Carlisle

Wednesday 14 September	Hunslet	v.	Batley
	Swinton	v.	Runcorn H.

Wednesday 21 September	Sheffield E.	v.	Mansfield M.

Sunday 25 September	Barrow	v.	Whitehaven
	Batley	v.	Hunslet
	Fulham	v.	Bramley
	Huddersfield	v.	Carlisle
	Leigh	v.	Sheffield E.
	Rochdale H.	v.	Keighley
	Runcorn H.	v.	Doncaster
	Swinton	v.	Mansfield M.
	Workington T.	v.	Chorley B.
	York	v.	Dewsbury

Sunday 2 October	Batley	v.	Huddersfield
	Bramley	v.	Swinton
	Carlisle	v.	Leigh
	Chorley B.	v.	Barrow
	Doncaster	v.	Dewsbury
	Keighley	v.	Workington T.
	Mansfield M.	v.	Hunslet
	Sheffield E.	v.	York
	Whitehaven	v.	Rochdale H.

Sunday 9 October	Barrow	v.	Keighley
	Carlisle	v.	Doncaster
	Chorley B.	v.	Sheffield E.
	Dewsbury	v.	Rochdale H.
	Fulham	v.	Batley
	Leigh	v.	Hunslet
	Runcorn H.	v.	Whitehaven
	Swinton	v.	York
	Workington T.	v.	Huddersfield

Sunday 16 October	Batley	v.	Mansfield M.
	Bramley	v.	Fulham
	Doncaster	v.	Workington T.
	Huddersfield	v.	Dewsbury
	Hunslet	v.	Barrow
	Keighley	v.	Carlisle
	Rochdale H.	v.	Chorley B.
	Sheffield E.	v.	Leigh
	Whitehaven	v.	Runcorn H.
	York	v.	Swinton

Sunday 23 October	Barrow	v.	Rochdale H.
	Carlisle	v.	Runcorn H.
	Chorley B.	v.	Bramley
	Dewsbury	v.	York
	Fulham	v.	Huddersfield
	Leigh	v.	Whitehaven
	Mansfield M.	v.	Doncaster
	Sheffield E.	v.	Batley
	Swinton	v.	Keighley

Sunday 30 October	Batley	v.	Rochdale H.
	Bramley	v.	Dewsbury
	Carlisle	v.	Barrow
	Huddersfield	v.	Workington T.
	Keighley	v.	Hunslet
	Mansfield M.	v.	Swinton
	Runcorn H.	v.	Fulham
	Whitehaven	v.	Chorley B.
	York	v.	Leigh

Sunday 6 November	Barrow	v.	Swinton
	Batley	v.	Carlisle
	Chorley B.	v.	Runcorn H.
	Fulham	v.	York
	Hunslet	v.	Dewsbury
	Leigh	v.	Mansfield M.
	Rochdale H.	v.	Huddersfield
	Sheffield E.	v.	Keighley
	Workington T.	v.	Doncaster

Sunday 20 November	Chorley B.	v.	Carlisle
	Dewsbury	v.	Workington T.
	Doncaster	v.	Hunslet
	Huddersfield	v.	Sheffield E.
	Leigh	v.	Bramley
	Mansfield M.	v.	Fulham
	Runcorn H.	v.	Rochdale H.
	Whitehaven	v.	Batley
	York	v.	Barrow
Sunday 4 December	Barrow	v.	Leigh
	Batley	v.	Runcorn H.
	Bramley	v.	Mansfield M.
	Carlisle	v.	Dewsbury
	Chorley B.	v.	Whitehaven
	Hunslet	v.	Huddersfield
	Keighley	v.	Swinton
	Workington T.	v.	Fulham
	York	v.	Doncaster
Sunday 11 December	Dewsbury	v.	Mansfield M.
	Doncaster	v.	Bramley
	Fulham	v.	Hunslet
	Keighley	v.	Sheffield E.
	Leigh	v.	Carlisle
	Rochdale H.	v.	Batley
	Runcorn H.	v.	Huddersfield
	Swinton	v.	Workington T.
	Whitehaven	v.	Barrow
	York	v.	Chorley B.
Sunday 18 December	Barrow	v.	Runcorn H.
	Batley	v.	Fulham
	Carlisle	v.	Swinton
	Hunslet	v.	Keighley
	Mansfield M.	v.	Leigh
	Sheffield E.	v.	Dewsbury
	Workington T.	v.	Rochdale H.
	York	v.	Bramley
Monday 26 December Boxing Day	Barrow	v.	Carlisle
	Bramley	v.	Hunslet
	Chorley B.	v.	Leigh
	Dewsbury	v.	Batley
	Doncaster	v.	Sheffield E.
	Huddersfield	v.	Runcorn H.
	Rochdale H.	v.	Swinton
	Whitehaven	v.	Workington T.
	York	v.	Mansfield M.
1989 Sunday 1 January New Year's Day	Batley	v.	Dewsbury
	Carlisle	v.	Whitehaven
	Doncaster	v.	Huddersfield
	Fulham	v.	Rochdale H.
	Hunslet	v.	York
	Keighley	v.	Bramley
	Leigh	v.	Swinton
	Runcorn H.	v.	Chorley B.
	Workington T.	v.	Barrow
Monday 2 January	Mansfield M.	v.	Sheffield E.
Sunday 8 January	Barrow	v.	Hunslet
	Bramley	v.	Batley
	Carlisle	v.	Fulham
	Chorley B.	v.	Keighley
	Dewsbury	v.	Doncaster
	Huddersfield	v.	Mansfield M.
	Leigh	v.	Workington T.
	Rochdale H.	v.	Runcorn H.
	Whitehaven	v.	Swinton
Sunday 15 January	Batley	v.	Sheffield E.
	Bramley	v.	Barrow
	Doncaster	v.	Carlisle
	Fulham	v.	Whitehaven
	Keighley	v.	Rochdale H.
	Mansfield M.	v.	Chorley B.
	Runcorn H.	v.	Leigh
	Swinton	v.	Hunslet
	Workington T.	v.	Dewsbury
	York	v.	Huddersfield
Sunday 22 January	Barrow	v.	Chorley B.
	Carlisle	v.	Rochdale H.
	Dewsbury	v.	Fulham
	Huddersfield	v.	Bramley
	Leigh	v.	Keighley
	Mansfield M.	v.	York
	Runcorn H.	v.	Workington T.
	Sheffield E.	v.	Swinton
	Whitehaven	v.	Doncaster
Sunday 5 February	Bramley	v.	Sheffield E.
	Carlisle	v.	Keighley
	Chorley B.	v.	Hunslet
	Dewsbury	v.	Whitehaven
	Doncaster	v.	Runcorn H.
	Fulham	v.	Mansfield M.
	Huddersfield	v.	York
	Rochdale H.	v.	Leigh
	Swinton	v.	Barrow
	Workington T.	v.	Batley
Sunday 19 February	Batley	v.	Doncaster
	Chorley B.	v.	Mansfield M.
	Hunslet	v.	Leigh
	Keighley	v.	York
	Rochdale H.	v.	Workington T.
	Runcorn H.	v.	Swinton
	Sheffield E.	v.	Huddersfield
	Whitehaven	v.	Fulham
Sunday 26 February	Carlisle	v.	Chorley B.
	Dewsbury	v.	Bramley
	Doncaster	v.	Rochdale H.
	Fulham	v.	Runcorn H.
	Huddersfield	v.	Whitehaven
	Leigh	v.	Barrow
	Mansfield M.	v.	Batley
	Swinton	v.	Sheffield E.
	Workington T.	v.	Keighley

The 1988–89 Fixtures

Sunday 5 March				Monday 27 March Easter Monday			
Barrow	v.	York		Barrow	v.	Workington T.
Batley	v.	Bramley		Bramley	v.	Keighley
Chorley B.	v.	Swinton		Chorley B.	v.	Rochdale H.
Fulham	v.	Workington T.		Dewsbury	v.	Huddersfield
Hunslet	v.	Mansfield M.		Doncaster	v.	Batley
Rochdale H.	v.	Dewsbury		Sheffield E.	v.	Fulham
Runcorn H.	v.	Carlisle		Swinton	v.	Leigh
Sheffield E.	v.	Doncaster		Whitehaven	v.	Carlisle
Whitehaven	v.	Keighley		York	v.	Hunslet

Sunday 12 March

Bramley	v.	Chorley B.
Dewsbury	v.	Carlisle
Doncaster	v.	Whitehaven
Huddersfield	v.	Batley
Leigh	v.	Rochdale H.
Mansfield M.	v.	Barrow
Sheffield E.	v.	Hunslet
Workington T.	v.	Runcorn H.
York	v.	Fulham

Sunday 2 April

Batley	v.	York
Bramley	v.	Leigh
Fulham	v.	Carlisle
Huddersfield	v.	Hunslet
Keighley	v.	Barrow
Mansfield M.	v.	Dewsbury
Rochdale H.	v.	Doncaster
Sheffield E.	v.	Chorley B.
Swinton	v.	Whitehaven

Sunday 19 March

Barrow	v.	Sheffield E.
Batley	v.	Workington T.
Carlisle	v.	Huddersfield
Chorley B.	v.	York
Hunslet	v.	Doncaster
Keighley	v.	Mansfield M.
Rochdale H.	v.	Fulham
Runcorn H.	v.	Dewsbury
Swinton	v.	Bramley
Whitehaven	v.	Leigh

Sunday 9 April

Barrow	v.	Bramley
Carlisle	v.	Workington T.
Dewsbury	v.	Sheffield E.
Doncaster	v.	Mansfield M.
Hunslet	v.	Fulham
Keighley	v.	Runcorn H.
Leigh	v.	York
Whitehaven	v.	Huddersfield

Friday 24 March Good Friday

Fulham	v.	Doncaster
Hunslet	v.	Bramley
Leigh	v.	Chorley B.
Runcorn H.	v.	Keighley
Swinton	v.	Rochdale H.
Workington T.	v.	Whitehaven
York	v.	Sheffield E.

Sunday 16 April

Batley	v.	Whitehaven
Bramley	v.	York
Fulham	v.	Dewsbury
Huddersfield	v.	Doncaster
Hunslet	v.	Sheffield E.
Mansfield M.	v.	Keighley
Rochdale H.	v.	Carlisle
Runcorn H.	v.	Barrow
Workington T.	v.	Swinton

The Rugby League Clubs Directory

Barrow

First season: 1900–01
Secretary: W. E. Livingstone
Coach: Rod Reddy
Colours: Royal blue and white jerseys, white shorts
Alternative colours: Red jerseys, red shorts
Ground address: Craven Park, Barrow-in-Furness. Tel.: 0229–20273
Nearest railway station: Barrow-in-Furness

Challenge Cup winners: 1954–55
Lancashire Cup winners: 1954–55, 1983–84
Division Two champions: 1975–76, 1983–84

Leading scorers 1987–88: Tries: 10 by Tony Kay
Goals: 27 by Steve Tickle
Points: 74 by Steve Tickle

Batley

First season: 1895–96
Secretary: L. Hardy
Coach: Paul Daley
Colours: Cerise and fawn hooped jerseys, cerise shorts
Alternative colours: Green jerseys, cerise shorts
Ground address: Mount Pleasant, Batley. Tel.: 0924–472208
Nearest railway station: Batley or Dewsbury

Challenge Cup winners: 1896–97, 1897–98, 1900–01
Yorkshire Cup winners: 1912–13
Championship winners: 1923–24

Leading scorers 1987–88: Tries: 8 by Simon Wilson
Goals: 24 by Damian McGrath
Points: 71 by Damian McGrath

Bradford Northern

First season: 1895–96
Secretary: J. Moses
Coach: Barry Seabourne
Colours: White jerseys with red, amber and black hoops, white shorts
Alternative colours: Red jerseys, white shorts
Ground address: Odsal Stadium, Bradford. Tel.: 0274–733899
Nearest railway station: Bradford

Challenge Cup winners: 1905–06, 1943–44, 1946–47, 1948–49
Yorkshire Cup winners: 1906–07, 1940–41, 1941–42, 1943–44, 1945–46, 1948–49,
        1949–50, 1953–54, 1965–66, 1978–79, 1987–88
John Player Trophy winners: 1974–75, 1979–80
Division One champions: 1903–04, 1979–80, 1980–81
Division Two champions: 1973–74
Premiership winners: 1977–78

Leading scorers 1987–88: Tries: 15 by Karl Fairbank
                     Goals: 80 by David Hobbs
                     Points: 180 by David Hobbs

Bramley

First season: 1896–97
Secretary: B. Rennison
Coach: Tony Fisher
Colours: Black jerseys with yellow V, black shorts
Alternative colours: Green jerseys, white shorts
Ground address: McLaren Field, Town Street, Bramley. Tel.: 0532–564842
Nearest railway station: Bramley

Leading scorers 1987–88: Tries: 17 by Peter Lister
                     Goals: 28 by Peter Lister
                     Points: 123 by Peter Lister

Carlisle

First season: 1981–82
Secretary: R. Taylor
Coach: Roy Lester
Colours: Royal blue jerseys with red and white band, red shorts
Alternative colours: Green jerseys with red and white band, red shorts
Ground address: Gillford Park, Petteril Bank Road, Carlisle. Tel.: 0228–26449
Nearest railway station: Carlisle

Leading scorers 1987–88: Tries: 22 by Kevin Pape
                     Goals: 56 by Brian Tunstall
                     Points: 110 by Brian Tunstall

Castleford

First season: 1926–27
Secretary: Mrs. D. Cackett
Coach: Darryl Van De Velde
Colours: Amber jerseys with black hoops, black shorts
Alternative colours: White jerseys with black and amber hoops, white shorts
Ground address: Wheldon Road, Castleford. Tel.: 0977–552674
Nearest railway station: Castleford

Challenge Cup winners: 1934–35, 1968–69, 1969–70, 1985–86
Yorkshire Cup winners: 1977–78, 1981–82, 1986–87
John Player Trophy winners: 1976–77

Leading scorers 1987–88: Tries: 13 by David Plange
                     Goals: 64 by Robert Beardmore
                     Points: 151 by Robert Beardmore

Chorley Borough

First season: 1954–55 (as Blackpool Borough; 1987–88 as Springfield Borough; 1988–89 as Chorley Borough)
Secretary: D. S. Brown
Coach: Mike Peers
Colours: Black and white jerseys, white shorts
Ground address: Victory Park, Duke St., Chorley. Tel.: 025 72–41349
Nearest railway station: Chorley
Leading scorers 1987–88: Tries: 11 by Carl Briscoe and Tommy Frodsham
                           Goals: 98 by Mike Smith
                           Points: 194 by Mike Smith

Dewsbury

First season: 1901–02
Secretary: G. W. Parrish
Coach: Terry Crook
Colours: Red, amber and black jerseys, white shorts
Alternative colours: Red jerseys, white shorts
Ground address: Crown Flatt, Leeds Road, Dewsbury. Tel.: 0924–465489
Nearest railway station: Dewsbury

Challenge Cup winners: 1911–12, 1942–43
Yorkshire Cup winners: 1925–26, 1927–28, 1942–43
Championship winners: 1972–73
Division Two champions: 1904–05

Leading scorers 1987–88: Tries: 11 by Chris Vasey
                           Goals: 71 by Chris Vasey
                           Points: 185 by Chris Vasey

Doncaster

First season: 1951–52
Secretary: G. Bowen
Coach: John Sheridan
Colours: White jerseys with blue and gold bands, white shorts
Alternative colours: Red jerseys, white shorts
Ground address: Bentley Road, Doncaster. Tel.: 0302–63756
Nearest railway station: Doncaster

Leading scorers 1987–88: Tries: 14 by Kevin Jones
                           Goals: 76 by David Noble
                           Points: 171 by David Noble

Featherstone Rovers

First season: 1921–22
Secretary: T. Jones
Coach: Peter Fox
Colours: Blue and white hooped jerseys, blue shorts
Alternative colours: Blue jerseys with white band, blue shorts
Ground address: Post Office Road, Featherstone. Tel.: 0977–702386
Nearest railway station: Wakefield Westgate & Wakefield Kirkgate

Challenge Cup winners: 1966–67, 1972–73, 1982–83
Yorkshire Cup winners: 1939–40, 1959–60
Division One champions: 1976–77
Division Two champions: 1979–80

Leading scorers 1987–88: Tries: 21 by Peter Smith
Goals: 128 by Steve Quinn
Points: 303 by Steve Quinn

Fulham

First season: 1980–81
Secretary: T. Lamb
Coach: Bev Risman
Colours: Black jerseys with red and white chevron, black shorts
Alternative colours: White jerseys with black and red chevron, red shorts
Ground address: Polytechnic of Central London Sports Ground, Great Chertsey Road,
    Chiswick, London W4. Tel.: 01–994 5817
Nearest railway station: Chiswick or Mortlake

Division Two champions: 1982–83

Leading scorers 1987–88: Tries: 9 by Dave Gillan
Goals: 40 by Colin Fenn
Points: 84 by Colin Fenn

Halifax

First season: 1895–96
Secretary: A. Beevers
Coaches: Graham Eadie and Ross Strudwick
Colours: Blue and white hooped jerseys, white shorts
Alternative colours: White jerseys with blue chevron, white shorts
Ground address: Thrum Hall, Halifax. Tel.: 0422–61026
Nearest railway station: Halifax

Challenge Cup winners: 1902–03, 1903–04, 1930–31, 1938–39, 1986–87
Yorkshire Cup winners: 1908–09, 1944–45, 1954–55, 1955–56, 1963–64
John Player Trophy winners: 1971–72
Championship winners: 1906–07, 1964–65
Division One champions: 1902–03, 1985–86

Leading scorers 1987–88: Tries: 17 by Tony Anderson and Paul Dixon
Goals: 75 by Colin Whitfield
Points: 175 by Colin Whitfield

Huddersfield

First season: 1895–96
Secretary: J. S. Greaves
Coaches: Neil Whittaker and Allen Jones
Colours: Claret and gold jerseys, black shorts
Alternative colours: White jerseys with claret and gold band
Ground address: Arena '84, Huddersfield. Tel.: 0484–530710
Nearest railway station: Huddersfield

Challenge Cup winners: 1912–13, 1914–15, 1919–20, 1932–33, 1944–45, 1952–53
Yorkshire Cup winners: 1909–10, 1911–12, 1913–14, 1914–15, 1918–19, 1919–20,
    1926–27, 1931–32, 1938–39, 1950–51, 1952–53, 1957–58
Championship winners: 1911–12, 1912–13, 1914–15, 1928–29, 1929–30, 1948–49,
    1961–62
Division Two champions: 1974–75

Leading scorers 1987–88: Tries: 10 by Ian Thomas
                    Goals: 41 by Simon Kenworthy
                    Points: 101 by Simon Kenworthy

Hull

First season: 1895–96
Secretary: M. Stanley
Coach: Brian Smith
Colours: Black and white irregular hooped jerseys, white shorts
Alternative colours: White jerseys with black trim
Ground address: The Boulevard, Airlie Street, Hull. Tel.: 0482–29040
Nearest railway station: Hull Paragon

Challenge Cup winners: 1913–14, 1981–82
Yorkshire Cup winners: 1923–24, 1969–70, 1982–83, 1983–84, 1984–85
John Player Trophy winners: 1981–82
Championship winners: 1919–20, 1920–21, 1935–36, 1955–56, 1957–58
Division One champions: 1982–83
Division Two champions: 1976–77, 1978–79

Leading scorers 1987–88: Tries: 14 by Gary Divorty
                    Goals: 111 by Gary Pearce
                    Points: 237 by Gary Pearce

Hull Kingston Rovers

First season: 1899–1900
Secretary: R. Turner
Coach: Roger Millward
Colours: White jerseys with red yoke and sleeves, white shorts
Alternative colours: Blue jerseys, white shorts
Ground address: Craven Park, Hull. Tel.: 0482–74648
Nearest railway station: Hull Paragon

Challenge Cup winners: 1979–80
Yorkshire Cup winners: 1920–21, 1929–30, 1966–67, 1967–68, 1971–72, 1974–75,
    1985–86
John Player Trophy winners: 1984–85
Championship winners: 1922–23, 1924–25
Division One champions: 1978–79, 1983–84, 1984–85
Premiership winners: 1980–81, 1983–84

Leading scorers 1987–88: Tries: 13 by Wayne Parker
                    Goals: 90 by Mike Fletcher
                    Points: 196 by Mike Fletcher

Hunslet

First season: 1895–96
Secretary: M. Grainger
Coach: Nigel Stephenson
Colours: Myrtle, white and flame jerseys, myrtle shorts
Alternative colours: White jerseys with myrtle and flame V, white shorts
Ground address: Elland Road, Leeds. Tel.: 0532–711675
Nearest railway station: Leeds City

Challenge Cup winners: 1907–08, 1933–34
Yorkshire Cup winners: 1905–06, 1907–08, 1962–63
Championship winners: 1907–08, 1937–38
Division Two champions: 1962–63, 1986–87

Leading scorers 1987–88 Tries: 8 by Jimmy Irvine
Goals: 61 by Alan Platt
Points: 140 by Alan Platt

Keighley

First season: 1901–02
Secretary: M. Lofthouse
Coach: Colin Dixon
Colours: White jerseys with scarlet and emerald green V, white shorts
Alternative colours: Red jerseys with white collar and cuffs, white shorts
Ground address: Lawkholme Lane, Keighley. Tel.: 0535–602602
Nearest railway station: Keighley

Division Two champions: 1902–03

Leading scorers 1987–88: Tries: 13 by Peter Richardson and Ricky Winterbottom
Goals: 63 by Carl Hirst
Points: 168 by Carl Hirst

Leeds

First season: 1895–96
Secretary: A. Davies
Coach: Malcolm Reilly
Colours: Blue and amber jerseys, white shorts
Alternative colours: White jerseys with blue and amber hoops, white shorts
Ground address: Headingley, Leeds. Tel.: 0532–786181
Nearest railway station: Leeds City

Challenge Cup winners: 1909–10, 1922–23, 1931–32, 1935–36, 1940–41, 1941–42, 1956–57, 1967–68, 1976–77, 1977–78
Yorkshire Cup winners: 1921–22, 1928–29, 1930–31, 1932–33, 1934–35, 1935–36, 1937–38, 1958–59, 1968–69, 1970–71, 1972–73, 1973–74, 1975–76, 1976–77, 1979–80, 1980–81
John Player Trophy winners: 1972–73, 1983–84
Championship winners: 1960–61, 1968–69, 1971–72
Premiership winners: 1974–75, 1978–79

Leading scorers 1987–88: Tries: 22 by Garry Schofield
Goals: 43 by David Creasser
Points: 142 by David Creasser

Leigh

First season: 1895–96
Secretary: J. A. Clark
Coach: Billy Benyon
Colours: Red jerseys with broad white band and black trim, white shorts
Alternative colours: Blue jerseys, white shorts
Ground address: Hilton Park, Leigh. Tel.: 0942–674437

Challenge Cup winners: 1920–21, 1970–71
Lancashire Cup winners: 1952–53, 1955–56, 1970–71, 1981–82
Championship winners: 1905–06
Division One champions: 1981–82
Division Two champions: 1977–78, 1985–86

Leading scorers 1987–88: Tries: 12 by John Kerr
Goals: 41 by Chris Johnson
Points: 88 by Chris Johnson

Mansfield Marksman

First season: 1984–85
Secretary: D. Parker
Coach: Billy Platt
Colours: Yellow and green jerseys, green shorts
Ground address: Sutton Town AFC, Low Moor Rd., Kirkby-in-Ashfield, Notts. Tel.:
0623–752181
Nearest railway station: Mansfield Parkway

Leading scorers 1987–88: Tries: 10 by Joe Warburton
Goals: 27 by Mick Howarth
Points: 74 by Mick Howarth

Oldham

First season: 1895–96
Secretary: Mrs. A. Lees
Coach: Eric Fitzsimons
Colours: Red and white hooped jerseys, blue shorts
Alternative colours: Blue and white hooped jerseys, blue shorts
Ground address: Watersheddings, Oldham. Tel.: 061–652 5244
Nearest railway station: Oldham Mumps

Challenge Cup winners: 1898–99, 1924–25, 1926–27
Lancashire Cup winners: 1907–08, 1910–11, 1913–14, 1919–20, 1924–25, 1933–34,
1956–57, 1957–58, 1958–59
Championship winners: 1909–10, 1910–11, 1956–57
Division One champions: 1904–05
Division Two champions: 1963–64, 1981–82, 1987–88
Second Division Premiership winners: 1987–88

Leading scorers 1987–88: Tries: 21 by Des Foy
Goals: 62 by Keith Atkinson and Peter Walsh
Points: 164 by Peter Walsh

Rochdale Hornets

First season: 1895–96
Secretary: P. Reynolds
Coach: Jim Crellin
Colours: White jerseys with red and blue band, white shorts
Alternative colours: Blue jerseys with red and white band, white shorts
Ground address: Spotland Stadium, Sandy Lane, Rochdale. Tel.: 0706–44698
Nearest railway station: Rochdale

Challenge Cup winners: 1921–22
Lancashire Cup winners: 1911–12, 1914–15, 1918–19

Leading scorers 1987–88: Tries: 12 by Andy Ruane
Goals: 41 by David Wood
Points: 84 by Andy Ruane and David Wood

Runcorn Highfield

First season: 1922–23 (as Wigan Highfield; 1933–34 as London Highfield; 1934–35 as Liverpool Stanley; 1951–52 as Liverpool City; 1968–69 as Huyton; 1984–85 as Runcorn Highfield)
Secretary: I. R. W. Swann
Coach: Bill Ashurst
Colours: Green jerseys with yellow V, green shorts
Alternative colours: Red jerseys with amber and black V, red shorts
Ground address: Canal Street, Runcorn. Tel.: 09285–66971
Nearest railway station: Runcorn

Leading scorers 1987–88: Tries: 11 by John Cogger
Goals: 45 by Terry Rose
Points: 126 by Terry Rose

St Helens

First season: 1895–96
Secretary: G. Sutcliffe
Coach: Alex Murphy
Colours: White jerseys with red V and red sleeves, white shorts
Alternative colours: Sky blue jerseys with navy blue sleeves and V, navy blue shorts
Ground address: Knowsley Road, St Helens. Tel.: 0744–23697
Nearest railway station: St Helens Central or St Helens Junction

Challenge Cup winners: 1955–56, 1960–61, 1965–66, 1971–72, 1975–76
Lancashire Cup winners: 1926–27, 1953–54, 1960–61, 1961–62, 1962–63, 1963–64, 1964–65, 1967–68, 1968–69, 1984–85
John Player Trophy winners: 1987–88
Championship winners: 1931–32, 1952–53, 1958–59, 1965–66, 1969–70, 1970–71
Division One champions: 1974–75
Premiership winners: 1975–76, 1976–77, 1984–85

Leading scorers 1987–88: Tries: 20 by Mark Elia
Goals: 111 by Paul Loughlin
Points: 254 by Paul Loughlin

Salford

First season: 1896–97
Secretary: G. McCarty
Coach: Kevin Ashcroft
Colours: Red jerseys with white chevron, white shorts
Alternative colours: White jerseys with red chevron, white shorts
Ground address: The Willows, Willows Road, Weaste, Salford. Tel.: 061–737 6363
Nearest railway station: Manchester Piccadilly or Manchester Victoria

Challenge Cup winners: 1937–38
Lancashire Cup winners: 1931–32, 1934–35, 1935–36, 1936–37, 1972–73
Championship winners: 1913–14, 1932–33, 1936–37, 1938–39
Division One champions: 1973–74, 1975–76

Leading scorers 1987–88: Tries: 13 by Steve Gibson
Goals: 79 by Ken Jones
Points: 194 by Ken Jones

Sheffield Eagles

First season: 1984–85
Secretary: Gary Hetherington
Coach: Gary Hetherington
Colours: Red, black and white jerseys, white shorts
Alternative colours: Dark blue jerseys, white shorts
Ground address: Owlerton Stadium, Sheffield. Tel.: 0742–337664
Nearest railway station: Sheffield

Leading scorers 1987–88: Tries: 14 by Steve Lidbury
Goals: 46 by Roy Rafferty
Points: 132 by Roy Rafferty

Swinton

First season: 1896–97
Secretary: S. R. Moyse
Coaches: Frank Barrow and Peter Smethurst
Colours: Blue jerseys with white V, white shorts
Alternative colours: White jerseys with blue V, white shorts
Ground address: Station Road, Swinton. Tel.: 061–794 1719
Nearest railway station: Swinton

Challenge Cup winners: 1899–1900, 1925–26, 1927–28
Lancashire Cup winners: 1925–26, 1927–28, 1939–40, 1969–70
Championship winners: 1926–27, 1927–28, 1930–31, 1934–35
Division One champions: 1962–63, 1963–64
Division Two champions: 1984–85
Second Division Premiership winners: 1986–87

Leading scorers 1987–88: Tries: 13 by Tex Evans
Goals: 67 by Paul Topping
Points: 150 by Paul Topping

Wakefield Trinity

First season: 1895–96
Secretary: G. Gledhill
Coach: David Topliss
Colours: White jerseys with red and blue band, white shorts
Alternative colours: Red jerseys with blue and white band, white shorts
Ground address: Belle Vue, Doncaster Road, Wakefield. Tel.: 0924–372445
Nearest railway station: Wakefield Westgate or Wakefield Kirkgate or Sandal and Agbrigg

Challenge Cup winners: 1908–09, 1945–46, 1959–60, 1961–62, 1962–63
Yorkshire Cup winners: 1910–11, 1924–25, 1946–47, 1947–48, 1951–52, 1956–57, 1960–61, 1961–62, 1964–65
Championship winners: 1966–67, 1967–68
Division Two champions: 1903–04

Leading scorers 1987–88: Tries: 20 by Mark Conway
Goals: 116 by Kevin Harcombe
Points: 244 by Kevin Harcombe

Warrington

First season: 1895–96
Secretary: R. Close
Coach: Tony Barrow
Colours: White jerseys with primrose and blue hoop, white shorts
Alternative colours: Blue jerseys with yellow trim, blue shorts
Ground address: Wilderspool Stadium, Warrington. Tel.: 0925–35338
Nearest railway stations: Warrington Central (Manchester and Liverpool line) or Warrington Bank Quay (main line)

Challenge Cup winners: 1904–05, 1906–07, 1949–50, 1953–54, 1973–74
Lancashire Cup winners: 1921–22, 1929–30, 1932–33, 1937–38, 1959–60, 1965–66, 1980–81, 1982–83
John Player Trophy winners: 1973–74, 1977–78, 1980–81
Championship winners: 1947–48, 1953–54, 1954–55
Premiership winners: 1985–86

Leading scorers 1987–88: Tries: 18 by Des Drummond
Goals: 153 by John Woods
Points: 352 by John Woods

Whitehaven

First season: 1948–49
Secretary: D. Farrell
Coach: Barry Smith
Colours: Chocolate, blue and gold jerseys, white shorts
Alternative colours: Red jerseys, blue shorts
Ground address: Recreation Ground, Coach Road, Whitehaven. Tel.: 0946–2915
Nearest railway station: Whitehaven

Leading scorers 1987–88: Tries: 14 by Mark Beckwith
Goals: 62 by Willie Richardson
Points: 176 by Willie Richardson

Widnes

First season: 1895–96
Secretary: J. Stringer
Coach: Doug Laughton
Colours: White jerseys, black shorts
Alternative colours: Red jerseys, red shorts
Ground address: Naughton Park, Widnes. Tel.: 051–424 2792
Nearest railway station: Widnes North

Challenge Cup winners: 1929–30, 1936–37, 1963–64, 1974–75, 1978–79, 1980–81, 1983–84
Lancashire Cup winners: 1945–46, 1974–75, 1975–76, 1976–77, 1978–79, 1979–80
John Player Trophy winners: 1975–76, 1978–79
Division One champions: 1977–78, 1987–88
Premiership winners: 1979–80, 1981–82, 1982–83, 1987–88

Leading scorers 1987–88: Tries: 42 by Martin Offiah
Goals: 63 by John Myler
Points: 168 by Martin Offiah

Wigan

First season: 1895–96
Secretary: Miss M. Charnock
Coach: Graham Lowe
Colours: Cherry and white hooped jerseys, white shorts
Alternative colours: Blue jerseys with white band, blue shorts
Ground address: Central Park, Wigan. Tel.: 0942–31321
Nearest railway stations: Wigan Wallgate or Wigan North West

Challenge Cup winners: 1923–24, 1928–29, 1947–48, 1950–51, 1957–58, 1958–59, 1964–65, 1984–85, 1987–88
Lancashire Cup winners: 1905–06, 1908–09, 1909–10, 1912–13, 1922–23, 1928–29, 1938–39, 1946–47, 1947–48, 1948–49, 1949–50, 1950–51, 1951–52, 1966–67, 1971–72, 1973–74, 1985–86, 1986–87, 1987–88
John Player Trophy winners: 1982–83, 1985–86, 1986–87
Championship winners: 1908–09, 1921–22, 1925–26, 1933–34, 1945–46, 1946–47, 1949–50, 1951–52, 1959–60
Division One champions: 1986–87
Premiership winners: 1986–87
Leading scorers 1987–88: Tries: 31 by Ellery Hanley
Goals: 59 by David Stephenson
Points: 138 by David Stephenson

Workington Town

First season: 1945–46
Secretary: J. G. Bell
Coach: Maurice Bamford
Colours: White jerseys with blue band, white shorts
Alternative colours: Red and white hooped jerseys, white shorts
Ground address: Derwent Park, Workington. Tel.: 0900–3609
Nearest railway station: Workington

Challenge Cup winners: 1951–52
Lancashire Cup winners: 1977–78
Championship winners: 1950–51

Leading scorers 1987–88: Tries: 7 by Colin Falcon and Paul Penrice
Goals: 56 by Dave Lowden
Points: 118 by Dave Lowden

York

First season: 1901–02
Secretary: I. Clough
Coach: Gary Stephens
Colours: Amber and black jerseys, black shorts
Alternative colours: Red jerseys, red shorts
Ground address: Wigginton Road, York. Tel.: 0904–34636
Nearest railway station: York

Yorkshire Cup winners: 1922–23, 1933–34, 1936–37
Division Two champions: 1980–81

Leading scorers 1987–88: Tries: 19 by Iain Wigglesworth
Goals: 63 by St. John Ellis
Points: 174 by St. John Ellis